God's
Shalom Project

Bernhard Ott

Translated by Timothy J. Geddert

Published in cooperation with
Mennonite World Conference

Good Books

Intercourse, PA 17534
800/762-7171
www.goodbks.com

God's Shalom Project is published in cooperation with Mennonite World Conference (MWC) and has been selected for its Global Anabaptist-Mennonite Shelf of Literature. MWC chooses one book each year and urges its member churches to translate and study the book, in an effort to develop a common body of literature.

Mennonite World Conference is an international fellowship of Christian churches who trace their beginning to the 16th-century Radical Reformation in Europe, particularly to the Anabaptist movement. Today, more than 1,200,000 believers belong to this faith family; at least 55 percent are African, Asian, or Latin American.

MWC represents 87 Mennonite and Brethren in Christ national churches from 48 countries on five continents.

Creating a "space" is a primary ministry of MWC—where member churches experience communion, interdependence, solidarity, and mutual accountability. MWC provides occasions and networks, publications and exchanges where Mennonites and Brethren in Christ can experience fellowship and be encouraged to live and act more faithfully.

MWC intends to serve as a "global congregation," believing that the church is a worldwide body where people of different cultures and nations are "no longer strangers . . . but members of God's household . . . " (Ephesians 2:19).

MWC's headquarters are in Strasbourg, France. For more information, visit its website at www.mwc-cmm.org.

Noah and the dove. Early Christian fresco.
Location : Catacomb of SS. Marcellino e Pietro, Rome, Italy
Photo Credit : Scala / Art Resource, NY
Image Reference : ART128987

Design by Dawn J. Ranck

GOD'S SHALOM PROJECT
Copyright © 2004 by Good Books, Intercourse, PA 17534
International Standard Book Number: 1-56148-462-8
Library of Congress Catalog Card Number: 2004020665

Library of Congress Cataloging-in-Publication Data
Ott, Bernhard.
[Schalom. English]
God's shalom project / Bernhard Ott ; translated by Timothy J. Geddert.
    p. cm.
"Published in cooperation with Mennonite World Conference."
Includes bibliographical references.
ISBN 1-56148-462-8 (pbk. : alk. paper) 1. Bible--Theology. I. Title.
BS543.O88 2004
231.7'6--dc22   2004020665

Table of Contents

Acknowledgments

This book could not have been written without the inspiration of many people.

First of all, I owe thanks to my teachers who opened my eyes and my heart to the Bible, especially to biblical theology. Special thanks goes to Elmer Martens who taught me Old Testament theology in *God's Design* (North Richland Hills, TX: D&F Scott Publishing, Inc., 1998).

Gerd Theissen's book, *The Shadow of the Galilean* (Philadelphia, PA: Fortress Press, 1987), gave me inspiration for the format of the dialogue section at the end of each chapter.

The definition of the concept of *Shalom* as I introduce it in Chapter 2 was generated by an article by the German Old Testament scholar Otto Betz, *"Der Friede Gottes in einer friedlosen Welt,"* in *Theologische Auseinandersetzung mit dem Denken unserer Zeit,* Vol. 2 (Neuhausen-Stuttgart, 1984, 57).

I thank Mennonite World Conference for choosing this book as its 2004 selection for its Global Anabaptist/Mennonite Shelf of Literature. It is an honor, and I hope the book serves well in that capacity.

Special thanks to Timothy J. Geddert for providing such a lucid and readable English translation of my original German text.

Thank you, too, to Phyllis Pellman Good and to Merle Good of Good Books for editing and publishing *God's Shalom Project* in English.

Bernhard Ott
Liestal, Switzerland, July, 2004

Preface

Traditional churches lament that members are leaving in droves. Yet at the same time, mysticism, meditation, and charismatic church services are booming. People are experiencing a growing fascination with spiritual experiences. They spend vacation time in monasteries; they take pilgrimages; they practice various forms of meditative prayer—all postmodern forms of piety. People cook up their own forms of post-Christian private religion, fabricating individual religious systems out of building materials lying around in abundance. There's a veritable cafeteria of choices out there, and we can select the ideas we like to assemble theological ideas to suit our fancy; the choices are endless.

That is precisely why this book, *God's Shalom Project*, is so timely. It is not a cheap guide to the religious supermarket of theological ideas. I have searched long and hard for books that faithfully present the biblical story and at the same time speak a clear message to our present situation. This is the book I have been looking for! Here the heart of the Bible's message is opened up for the reader. And yet ideas are not over-simplified. Portraying the central message of the Scriptures can often be a challenge; there are texts that don't slide easily into place, and we are not well-served by theological systems that ignore or distort unruly texts. Bernhard Ott writes as a faithful biblical theologian, resisting the temptation to make everything conform to a completely harmonized system.

God's Shalom Project is a helpful resource for home fellowship groups, Bible study groups, Sunday school classes, and personal Bible study. During the past few years I have often found myself in conversation with people who have no religious background whatsoever. Over and over again I discover that such people consider the Bible to be a strange and confusing book, with no relevance for day-to-day life. Thanks to this book by Bernhard Ott, this situation has changed for some of them. Ott has managed to take the biblical story of God's dealings with humankind and make it connect with the secular reader. Biblical concepts and illustrations come alive and are made to seem familiar. God's good purposes become transparent and comprehensible. Even readers already familiar with the Bible will gain a deeper appreciation for the words and deeds of God. We find in this book a rich treasure house of biblical details and help in seeing the interconnectedness of those ideas.

While working through *God's Shalom Project,* I was reminded again that my few years on this earth are only a small segment of a much larger and longer story that stretches in both directions far beyond the borders of my birth and death. I have been intentionally placed in time for a specific purpose, and the journey is short. Yet at the end of it, there is a loving Father waiting for my return. I am no longer threatened by the prospect of death. And it is possible to understand things this way only when my life is seen as a journey toward the One who placed me here and who loves me without measure.

Ruedi Josuran, radio journalist
Stäfa, Switzerland

1.
When your children ask you . . .

Welcome!

God has a project. God invites us to be co-workers in this project. That is why I am a Christian . . . and an enthusiastic one at that! How regrettable when being a Christian is portrayed as something boring, something disengaged from the real world, or mere theory. If the God of the Bible has invited humans to participate in God's great plan for the universe, then God is certainly not interested in merely teaching humans boring theology.

Unfortunately there are lots of people who call themselves Christian, who speak of a personal relationship with Jesus, but have only a vague idea of what God's plans and goals are. Many have come to Christ because they have been concerned about the salvation of their souls. They have experienced conversion, and that's enough to give them security about their eternal destiny. And yet many of them have almost no clue about what God's great project is, nor how, since the creation of the earth, humans have been drawn into the fulfillment of God's plan. Nor do they understand how God deals with humans as they are drawn into the project of fulfilling this plan.

Sometimes it is the reverse . . . People are fascinated by the teaching of Jesus (for example the Sermon on the Mount) and with great passion set out to change the world. But with the passing of time, their energies drain away and they give up their goals with resignation. What is missing is a personal relationship with Jesus Christ. Have these people understood any better than the others what God's plans and purposes for humanity really are?

This book is about God's project. Its goal is to motivate and invite people to a joyful and committed Christian life.

Bible doctrine? Or telling the story?

What is the Christian faith about? How are we to summarize briefly and forthrightly the main truths of Scripture? I've been working with these questions now for over 25 years. Teaching the Bible has always been at the center of my heart. Whether as a children's Sunday school teacher, as a writer of Sunday school material for a denomination, as a Bible school or Bible college teacher, or as a preacher or conference speaker in many places—I have always been seeking to present basic biblical truths in interesting and fascinating ways so that people are invited to become part of God's project.

Always, a key question for me has been: **How can the old message be told in a new situation without losing its abiding truth, but in a way that speaks with freshness and relevance?** My question concerns not only the content of the Bible's teaching, but also the way it is passed on. How are the teachings of the Bible passed on most effectively?

When Israelite children asked their parents, "What is our faith all about? Why do we live as we do? Why do we pray? Why do we worship as we do?" their parents did not respond:

First, this is what God is like . . .

Second, we human beings are like this . . .

Third, this is what happens when we sin . . .

Fourth, we are supposed to understand God's commandments like this . . .

Fifth . . .

Rather than learning creeds and catechisms, **the children
were told stories!**[1] In fact they were told *the* story . . .

> *We were slaves in Egypt, but then God did a miracle, bringing
> us out of Egypt and setting us free. God forged us into a communi-
> ty, a community that would hold together through thick and thin.
> God told us how we were supposed to live—how to live successful-
> ly. And then God led us along the road toward the Promised Land,
> to the land in which we would live according to the pattern God
> had showed us. There we would be able to live happy and con-
> tented lives, no longer as slaves, but as people set free. And all the
> nations around us would be astonished and say, "What a great and
> wise God their God must be!" All along the way our God has pro-
> tected us from danger, met all our needs, given us food and drink.
> You see, that is why we pray and worship our God and live accord-
> ing to the pattern God gave us. That is what real life is all about.*

The Bible is not a theology textbook full of definitions of God
and the world, but rather a fascinating narrative, telling a not-yet-
finished story of God's ongoing dealings with people throughout
history. And we are all invited to be a part of this story.

How to use this book

This book has its origins in real-life experiences and was
designed to be used in real-life situations. This also explains its
structure.

Telling the story

For years I have attempted to retell the stories of God's dealings with humanity in many different kinds of situations. I've

tried to tell them in succinct and captivating ways. These stories, which contribute to our understanding of God's project, make up the beginning of each chapter in this book.

Thinking along and discussing

Yet this book is designed to invite readers to think beyond what is written. Each chapter contains questions designed to facilitate personal reflection and/or group study.

Perhaps the reader will sometimes ask: "Where do we find this in the Bible? How might Bernhard defend such an idea? Where did this notion come from?" And sometimes readers will disagree with what is written. At least that has often happened in the past as I have shared these ideas. And when that happens, interesting discussions often follow. Sometimes I have only needed to clarify what I meant, and these clarifications, in turn, have often found their way into the footnotes of this book.

Sometimes, however, the material here has led to lively debates about theological issues or about the practical implications of what I have written. My goal is also to motivate discussions and debates among those who read this book. Many of the questions that have been asked by past hearers have been incorporated at the end of each chapter into a fictional "letter exchange." Hopefully this dialogue will also encourage you to think more deeply about these matters or will lead to good discussions in study groups.

And now I invite you to a journey through the Bible that just might change your life.

---

1 Deuteronomy 6:20-25. (I will not always follow exactly any particular translation. Sometimes I will put the text into my own words, following closely well-known translations, or, where it seems important to do so, I will more literally reproduce the original text.)

2.
God has a project

The will of God

"Your kingdom come. Your will be done." These are words from the Lord's Prayer. Yet some might legitimately ask, "The will of God?[2] What is that? Who knows God's will? *Can* we know God's will?"

When God called Abraham, God said, "I will make of you a great nation, and I will bless you."[3] At the burning bush, God's self-revelation to Moses included the words, "I have observed the misery of my people. I have come down to deliver them." Later, when Moses asked about this again, he was given a precise answer: "I will free you and deliver you. I will take you as my people, and I will be your God. I will bring you into the land."[4] And that is how it goes through the entire Bible, right through to the vision of John who wrote: "Then I saw a new heaven and a new earth."[5] God does have a will, a plan, a goal. God has a project.

"In the beginning"—this is how the Bible's story begins. And in the book of Revelation history is straining toward its goal. Human history, according to the biblical perspective, has a beginning and it has an ultimate goal. It is not an endless cycle, as many religions would view it. At the beginning is God's creative word; God determines the beginning. And God has a goal, a plan, *a project,* as I will call it in what follows.

Our goal will be to gain some insight into God's project. Even a short introduction to God's purposes and goals can give our Christian life a new perspective.

But what is God's project?

In Psalm 85:9 we read that God wills peace *(Shalom)*. For this reason I call God's plan the *"Shalom* project." Contrary to what some might think, the Hebrew word *Shalom* has a much broader meaning than our word "peace."

Shalom has to do with payment. A look at a Hebrew lexicon reveals that *Shalom* is derived from the verb *shillem,* which means "to pay." One might say that there is *Shalom* when payment has been made, when there is no more debt. The Hebrew greeting *"sha'al shalom"* is not merely a wish for peace; it is actually a question: "Is there *Shalom,* or are there still debts to be paid?" Or paraphrased: "Are you happy to see me, or do I still owe you something?" If there is still a debt to be paid, there is not yet *Shalom.* But debts can be paid, and *Shalom* can return again.

But what if a debt is so great that it can never be paid? The only two solutions then, according to ancient Hebrew culture, are for someone to intervene and pay the *"Shalom* price" in place of the debtor, or else for the debt to be forgiven. In the Old Testament, God's people knew various institutions designed to restore *Shalom* by means of *"Shalom* price."[6]

But we all know that financial debts are not the only kinds of debts people owe. Humans cause injuries, pain, and injustices that cannot be reconciled with money alone. In situations like these, forgiveness is needed. That implies that people are released from the debts they owe and are not punished for having incurred them in the first place.

Shalom had another dimension in Israel beyond issues of payment. The relationship between humans and God is described with this concept. If everything is right between people and God, then there is *Shalom*. However, the Bible bears constant witness to the fact that things are not always right between people and God. Humans fell from their original relationship with the Creator and now do what they wish, not even listening to God's good voice. They have become debtors. How can *Shalom* be restored between humans and God? This, too, is what the biblical story is all about.

In sum: When things are the way they are supposed to be in human life, *Shalom* exists. There is *Shalom* when we can look God in the eye and know there is no guilt or debt. There is *Shalom* when we as humans can look each other in the eye and ask, "Are you happy to see me? Or is there still something between us?" and we can answer with a laugh: "Everything is right between us!" In fact, *Shalom* even means that we can "look *creation* in the eye"—God's good creation in which we live.

Often we find ourselves far from this ideal. And we long for a life of *Shalom*. We want a life in which everything is "right." And that's what life was meant to be. God wants this, too. This is what God's project is all about. This is what God is at work to accomplish. In fact, the story of the Bible is at its heart the story of God on a journey with humans on the way of *Shalom*. It is an invitation to join God again and again on this journey.

2 Matthew 6:6-13.
3 Genesis 12:2, 3.
4 Exodus 3:7ff; 6:6-8.
5 Revelation 21:1.
6 For example, there was the liberation of slaves and the remission of debts in the Jubilee Year (Leviticus 25). Compare also the parable of the unforgiving slave in Matthew 18:23-35.

For further reflection

1. How do I understand the word "peace"? What does peace include for me? How does my understanding of peace differ from the biblical meaning of peace (*Shalom*) described above?

2. Do I live in hope that there will one day be true peace in this world?

3. Are our churches instruments of God's peace? How can they become increasingly so?

4. Where am I at the present time involved in situations of conflict? How am I experiencing the conflict? What steps need to be taken in the direction of peace?

5. Why is peace so endangered? What makes us fail so often to live peacefully?

6. What do I hope to gain from a biblical study of this theme?

A Note to the readers: I am a teacher, and I like the give-and-take of the classroom. I miss that when I write a book. So I've created two imaginary readers—young students—who have questions about what I've written.

In my letters to them, I try to address their concerns and questions. I'm imagining the kinds of conversation, you, the reader, and I might have if we were sharing a classroom together.

Dear Monica and Peter,

I just read your letter with your first comments on the "*Shalom* project." You took seriously my encouragement to deepen your understanding of what you read by means of your own considerations.

Obviously you are having some trouble with my "*Shalom* fad" as you call it. You are even asking whether I am somewhat out of style. After all, the high point of the "peace movement" is long gone. Presumably you consider me a leftover (and gray-haired) representative of the "give-peace-a-chance" generation.

Well, let me put you at ease—or maybe make you even more uneasy. I did not arrive at this topic through the peace movement or any other movement for that matter. I arrived at it through a careful study of the Bible. In fact, that study didn't even require a great deal of effort. Just look in a Bible concordance at words like "peace," "reconciliation," and "justice," and you will be amazed. If you were then to check Greek and Hebrew lexicons, you would be positively astonished. Since I did that, I certainly no longer believe that topics like peace and justice are merely recent fashions. On the contrary, as you yourselves say, the topic of "peace" has slipped again into the background. Fashions come and go. And for that very reason the topic of peace dare not be made dependent on passing fads. If God addresses this theme in the Bible from beginning to end, how can we be silent about it?

Of course you are right; one could use other titles for the biblical story. Many theologians have suggested suitable ones. Some have identified *Covenant* as the main theme. Others have suggested the *Reign of God.* And still others interpret the Bible in terms of *Promise and Fulfillment.* These are all good titles as well.

I won't take the time here to explain in detail why I have decided in favor of the term *Shalom.* That's in fact what this whole book is designed to do. I can only invite you to keep reading and thinking about it. At the end we can discuss again whether *Shalom* is a suitable choice, if we want to summarize God's message in one word.

'Til next time,
Bernhard

3.
In the beginning

A good plan

We search in vain in the Bible's opening pages for the word *Shalom*. But we find another way of speaking of it, an expression which describes well what will later be called *Shalom*. As the work of creation was brought to completion, God said, "It is very good!"[7] God's creative work succeeded. It turned out as God had planned it. It was functional, harmonious, suited to the goals God had in mind. Let's take a closer look at precisely what was called "very good."

God's blueprint for humanity

Humanity is nothing special . . . just matter. We are made of the same stuff as the rest of creation—out of the "red field dirt," the Bible says.[8] That's why one Bible interpreter calls humanity simply "earthlings." A chemist who analyzed the material substance of a human and calculated its value suggests the human body is worth around five dollars. Really nothing special.

At the same time, humans are something magnificent, a wonderful masterpiece of the creator—not the product of chance, but the result of a very good plan. Humanity is also not a half-god, made out of a special "spiritual substance," as some ancient religions thought. No, humanity is God's wonderful creature, part of the created order. Humanity's very existence originates in the will of God, who created everything.

The biblical text uses the expression "living creature" to describe humanity,[9] the same expression used elsewhere to describe animals.[10] Humanity is indeed related to all other living creatures. Humans are creatures with needs, able to exist only when taking in air and nourishment. Yet at the same time, these needy creatures are ingenious "machines" in which fascinating processes of biology, chemistry, and physics are at work. Functioning, pulsing life is a mystery, understood only by our creator. And God says: This also is very good!

And then comes that which is unique. Psalm 8 puts it this way: "You have made them a little lower than God, and crowned them with glory and honor. You have given them dominion over the works of your hands; you have put all things under their feet." The first chapter of the Bible uses other words to say the same thing. Humanity was created in the image of God. No, that doesn't mean that God and humans have the same external appearance. The real meaning concerns the mandate God gave to humans. Humans are to be God's representatives, God's custodians in creation. Humanity has been called to a great assignment. The creation account in Scripture uses four expressions to define this assignment more explicitly: have dominion over, subdue, use, and protect.

Humanity has been commissioned, as a responsibility to God, to see to it that God's creation remains functional. God entrusted the creation into the hands of humanity; we have been called to be God's "trustees." That is why humans were created with the ability to think and to shape the world.

Humans can create culture. And God says, "This, too, is very good."

Another observation: Humans do not exist alone, as individual people. Adam ("man") in Genesis 1:26, 27 really means "humanity."[11] It is not the individual human, but the human community that is created in God's image. It is not the individual human, but the human community, male and female, that is entrusted with the role of custodian in God's creation. Humans are creatures in relationship. Humans require the help and complementarity of others.[12] And God says, "This, too, is very good."

And not least, humans are creatures who exist in God's presence. They can talk to God; they can enter a personal relationship with God. Humanity is God's very special creature. And God says, "This, too, is very good."

This is all good because it all belongs together—it fits together harmoniously. Humanity as creature and representative of God, humanity as individuals and as people in community, humanity in relationship to God and in relationship with the rest of creation, humanity as thinker and as feeler, humanity as ruler and servant, humanity as woman and humanity as man. There, wherever all of that fits together in harmony, is where it is very good. There is *Shalom*. This is God's plan, God's project.

---

7 Genesis 1.

8 Genesis 2:7 (compare also vv. 3:19, 23). The Hebrew word *"adama"* means "field dirt." The name "Adam" is derived from this, meaning "the one taken from the field dirt."

9 Genesis 2:7. The Hebrew word *"nephesh haja"* has sometimes been translated "living soul," a translation that leads to misunderstanding. "Living creature" is a better translation.

10 Genesis 1:20, 24, 30; 6:17; 7:15; 9:10.

11 "Adam" is here used as a collective concept (humanity), just as, for example, "man/humanity" in Ephesians 2:15.

12 Genesis 1:27 and 2:18-23.

For further reflection

1. How does the concept of "humanity" presented here fit together with the way I usually think of humanity? Are there aspects of it that are new or foreign to me?

2. Our concept of humanity has consequences for the way we live. Can I think of concrete examples of this? In marriage, perhaps? In male and female relationships? In the training of children? In my profession? In technology? In science? In psychology and medicine? In religion?

3. What does it mean that humanity is created in the "image of God"? How does this influence the way I think of myself as a human? Does it affect the way I live? The way I treat other people?

4. After considering these things, what would I like to tell God in prayer?

Dear Monica and Peter,

I'm glad to read that you are taking up the Bible yourselves and reading the texts to which I refer.

Now you write that you felt pretty insecure when I located humanity so near to "nature," so near to the "field-dirt" and the animals. Above all you took note that in your Bible, Genesis 2:7 says the first human was made into a "living soul." So it isn't hard for me to understand why you ask whether I think animals also have souls.

Did you really read Genesis 2:7 carefully? Does it really say that humans have living souls? No, it says that the first human became a living soul. You can understand why the word "soul" as we use it really is not suitable for what Genesis 2:7 wants to say. The text is not talking about a soul that can be distinguished from the body and that constitutes the "real person." That's how the Greeks understood the human person, but not the Hebrews. If we want to use the word "soul," then we should not use it to refer to something that a person *has*, but rather something that a person *is*. Through God's breath we were made into living beings, and in terms of "being souls," we are like the animals. Just read Genesis 1:20, 24; 7:15; 9:10. In all these texts the same expression is used for animals. They also are "souls," or to put it into language that we understand better today, "living creatures."

Besides, it is very meaningful to understand ourselves as part of the whole creation—the earth, the air, the water, the plant and animal world. The harmony of all God's creation is included in the concept of *Shalom*. Maybe we would take better care of God's creation if we were more aware that we belong to it for better and for worse. We are not magically spared if everything else—earth, water, air, plants, and animals—are destroyed. We are part of the larger system. We belong to creation. This is no new insight and certainly no invention of the 21st century. It is presented this way already in the biblical creation account.

Of course we don't want to forget the other side, that humanity is also something special. Humans are to be distinguished from all other living creatures and from creation as a whole in their relationship to God and their commission to be stewards of creation—but I already talked about that in the text.

So now I will leave you to keep working on the next chapter, curious about how you will respond to it.

Sincerely,
Bernhard

4.
People
are not robots

We live in an age of computers and robots. We program our machines and they do what we tell them. Are humans also machines of this type? Did God program humanity so that it would faithfully carry out the task of caring for the created world? Did God create robots for the task?

There is an advantage to having robots, of course. They do what they are told. But people are not like that. They are real, self-directing beings. They can listen, evaluate, differentiate, and decide. They can think; they can be creative; they can determine their own actions. Why did God make people like this? Wouldn't God have been able to avoid a great deal of frustration if God had created robots instead? God chose not to. Genesis 3-11 shows us what this means for human history.

The road that people chose

Because we are not robots, we can choose. Isn't that wonderful? We can decide. The first chapters of the Bible describe how God gave humanity an assignment. Humans are to be God's trustees; they are to be stewards of God's creation.

God's *Shalom* Project

In order to fulfill this assignment, humans were given both abilities and boundaries. God would always be the final authority. The knowledge of good and evil—that is to say, complete knowledge and ultimate decisions—are beyond the boundaries of human competence. Humans are stewards; but they are *only* stewards. They are not God.

If we were mere robots, some things might be a lot simpler. But because we are human, we can think and we can dream. And the snake is there to help us! "What would it be like if I were the boss?" passes through our minds. "These things God has been saying—are they really all true? Maybe God just wants to keep something from me to make sure I stay in check? Maybe God doesn't really have my best interests in mind?"

And because humans are in fact thinking beings, they can freely decide to be stewards of God's creation, or they can decide differently.

Everything we have always associated with "The Temptation" and with "The Fall" is normally considered horrible, awful. But could a positive side be seen in these as well? Robots cannot be tempted. There is no "Fall" for a computer. It is part of human dignity and human greatness to *decide*. And humans have decided. They have decided to take things into their own hands. They have decided not to be stewards, but to be bosses instead. Humans have decided in favor of autonomy.[13] And in so doing, humans have decided against God, their creator. They have broken faith with their Lord. And that is what the Bible calls sin. Sin is far more than doing bad deeds. Sin is revolt, unfaithfulness, rebellion. Humans have become rebels against God.

And after this decision comes a second—the decision against fellow human beings. It is the decision to go it alone, to be lord of creation, often at the expense of others. Brother kills brother; one human does away with another. This, too, belongs to "The Fall." And this is not only ancient history. It is still our fate today.

We, too, stand before God and face great decisions. Will we accept God's foreordained role for us as stewards of creation? Or will we choose autonomy? Will we recognize our own boundaries and limitations and choose to live in fellowship with others? Or will we choose our own way? The ability to choose brings with it responsibility. This is something humans must learn and something they *do* learn. For better or worse, decisions have consequences.

The consequences

"Where are you, Adam?" asks God. And not long after comes the second question: "Where is your brother, Cain?" These are the two great questions of human accountability. As humans we are not quite as alone as we sometimes think we are (and sometimes *wish* we were). As humans we must give an account. We cannot escape our roles as stewards and trustees. We are accountable to our Lord, whether we like it or not. When God asks the great questions, we must answer. And here again we can make a decision. We can say, "Here I am. I have become a rebel. I have stepped outside the boundaries. I've overestimated myself." But the first chapters of the Bible speak of what we do instead. We hide from God. We push blame on others, God, the serpent. And when asked about our brother, our sister, we answer with indifference. "Am I my brother's keeper? Do I always have to watch out for my sister?"

The results are tragic. We get what we choose. Just look at Cain. Without God, without a home, he wanders about the earth, longingly searching for a lost paradise. It looks like God's

God's *Shalom* Project

Shalom project has come to an end. True *Shalom*, true peace, has disappeared from all areas of life. The original harmony has fallen apart. No longer can we say, "Behold, it is very good!"

We look for love and find domination and oppression. We look for community and find war. We want to work but end up dealing with thorns and thistles. We work toward progress, but the effort leads us ever farther from God. We long for peace among nations and find more and more conflict. Genesis not only describes what humanity experienced thousands of years ago. It is the story of human history. It is the story of humanity in rebellion against God. It is the wistful story of human longing. It is the story of exhausted humanity, pushing the creator out of creation.

So what does God do?

The first 11 chapters of the Bible don't tell us very much about God's response. But the little that is said is enough to make one thing perfectly clear: God does not give up on rebels. The first evidence is simply the fact that humanity is not destroyed. In fact, God offers humanity protection and a place to live. God preserves Noah and his family and makes a binding covenant. These are signs that God has not rejected the rebels. And because God does not give up on the rebels, God also goes the second mile . . . graciously trying to win them back.

God's goal is always the restoration of *Shalom*. But of course the rebels must come back willingly—not as robots, but as people. God's project is to make people truly human again, human in the way God intended humanity to be: stewards in God's creation. What a project God is undertaking. Will God find humans willing to respond?

13 The Greek background of this word implies the meaning "living according to one's own law." This is the essence of sin. And it makes reference to the relationship between humans and God. Not all forms of autonomous behavior are to be considered sinful. Self-determination, in a psychological and sociological sense, can in fact be an important part of being human.

For further reflection

1. Why does the story of "The Fall" also have a positive side? What positive statement does it make about people?

2. Why is it important to understand sin not only as transgressing the law, but also as rebellion against God?

3. Where do I experience concretely in my life and surroundings the consequences of humankind trying to live without the creator?

4. What does restoration (winning back the rebels) really mean? What does it mean to say that God restores us? Do I let myself be won back to God?

5. What would I like to say to God in response to these thoughts?

Dear Monica and Peter,

You write that chapter 4 raised a few eyebrows. You are surprised that I can put such a positive spin on "The Fall." If I understand you correctly, you've always understood "The Fall" to mean only one thing: Humans are lost sinners.

I'm glad that you reacted as you did. That means you understood exactly what I wanted to say. Is it possible that you've previously read the story of "The Fall" only through a certain kind of "Christian lens" that sees humans only as bad, sinful, and evil? Of course I am not trying to eliminate this dark side. But the first chapters of the Bible (and not only these!) have a different story to tell as well. They speak of human freedom, of the ability to decide, of human dignity, of God taking humans very seriously. In fact, this topic will be continued in the very next chapter of this book.

I'm hearing you. You think I am overestimating humans, evaluating them far too optimistically. I guess there are dangers on both sides. Either we *overestimate* ourselves and then run the risk of making no room for God, understanding ourselves as free rulers of the world. Or else we *underestimate* ourselves and complain about our bondage, our sinfulness, our evil nature. Maybe we need to find a middle position between the two extremes. In fact, that would be the way to come closest to what the Bible says about us.

'Til next time,
Bernhard

5.
A new beginning

It was more than 30 years ago that Martin Luther King Jr., delivered his now famous sermon—"I Have A Dream!" In moving language he described his vision of a world community in which black and white could live together in peace, justice, and mutual love. This is an old dream, a biblical dream. It was God's intention for creation, for the human family. It was God's original *Shalom* project. Unfortunately, humans chose another way. But God does not start a project and then give up on it. Rather, God sticks with the project, starting over, if necessary—even if it has to be with one single human being and his family. We've reached the time of Abraham.[14]

The story of Abraham and his family is a story of good news. It is clear evidence of the fact that God did not give up on rebellious humanity. This story has a crucial role to play in the whole story of redemption, for God's great desire is to call humanity, runaway rebels, back home where they belong, in relationship with the creator.

The self-revealing God

Those who think that God is mute and absent . . . well, they've got it all wrong. The Abraham story makes very clear that God has not gone into hiding. After everything that

---

humanity, God's creation, has done, it would have been perfectly understandable if God had abandoned the great human project. But God does not turn away from humanity. People may try to hide from God, but God never gives up searching for the runaway rebels.

God's revelation contains a vision

God's project is again laid before humanity. We read in the Abraham story: "Go to a land that I will show you . . . I will make you the father of a great nation . . . All the peoples of the earth will be blessed through you."[15] Though God's new beginning focuses on one person, Abraham, it is designed to reach far beyond this one person.

God is not concerned merely with the personal salvation of one man, Abraham. God's plan is to make a great nation out of this one person and through this nation to bless all nations on earth. And here we begin to see glimpses of the universality of God's great project. God is not looking just for converted and born-again individuals. When people turn back to God, they also turn back to each other and to the rest of creation. And thus they return to their original creation mandate. This is the reason God presented Abraham with a vision that included both a nation and a new land.

It is the same in the New Testament. And it is the same today. The conversion of the individual is important. It is the starting point, but God is looking for more. God is looking for a people, a community of people, who will become a blessing to all people. And God is looking for a people who will steward creation according to God's plan. God wants a *Shalom* people, among whom harmony is restored, as it was in the beginning.

God's revelation contains a challenge

God begins with the individual; God's great vision is not simply thrown out over humanity as a collective. God created people as individuals, each with the ability to make decisions and take on responsibilities. And so God also takes each individual seriously. A specific person is called by name and invited to rejoin God's project. The text says, in effect: "Leave your home . . . move to a land that I will show you. This is my invitation. It is an invitation to begin a journey. Leave behind the old patterns of life; start out on something new, something you can't even imagine yet, but that I will certainly reveal to you." Isn't that astonishing? God does not start by piling up complaints and reproaches on rebellious humanity. Instead, God presents to humanity a magnificent vision of what life can be like. God pulls humanity out of the empty cycles of Babylonian religion and sets before humanity a vision of life's true goal. And then God invites humanity to set out on a journey toward that goal. It is the same today!

God's great plan for the church and for the Kingdom are not brought to fulfillment automatically, as if humanity sits passively while God makes it happen. No, God is looking for individuals, calling them by name, and inviting them to join God on a journey. Today, just as back then, God is about the business of planting in human hearts a vision for God's Kingdom of love, peace, and justice, inviting people to leave behind old habits and patterns of life, calling people away from emptiness and setting before them goals worth pursuing. Today, just as back then, God invites people to start out on the great adventure of a journey toward new life.

People can start over

The Abraham story reports simply: "Abraham listened to the call of God."[16] Over and over we hear people, especially Christians, say that humans are not capable of deciding in favor of what is good. But Abraham stands as an impressive example, right near the beginning of the Bible, that people can decide in favor of what is good.

And Abraham's example is one that provides a lot of hope. Don't write people off. Even when people have rebelled against God, even when they have turned totally away from God and gone their own way, there is still hope. When God calls and when God invites, people can respond. Over and over people have excused their unwillingness by claiming inability to choose any other way. The Abraham story teaches us something important. When God calls, it is indeed possible to answer.

Promise and fulfillment

People live in the tension between promise and fulfillment. Those who know the Abraham story know full well that God's promises are sometimes fulfilled only much later and after many hindrances have been overcome. The first and most natural setting in which God's *Shalom* project is to be fulfilled is in the family. If it had not been for Sarah, there would be no Abraham story. And yet even for Sarah, the path toward fulfillment led through doubt toward faith.[17]

Beyond the immediate family, God's *Shalom* project is also to be fulfilled in the extended family. Not that this is always easy. Living daily with his nephew Lot and Lot's family was not always easy for Abraham. Yet Abraham proved to be a man committed to *Shalom*, and he found a way to restore peace to his larger extended family.[18]

Finally, God's project was to extend far beyond one family. It contained the promise that Abraham's family would become a great nation. And yet Abraham and Sarah were growing old and this promise was not being fulfilled. They waited and waited, and, before their lives ended, that great nation consisted of exactly one son. They lived in this tension.

Daily they saw a vision of the promise. And daily they were challenged anew to follow faithfully in the way God was leading them. God had made a binding covenant with Abraham and he in turn was invited to be true to God.

We all live in the same tension. God has put a great vision before us. In fact, God's great *Shalom* project is still a vision out there ahead of us. God's Kingdom is still coming. We are heading toward the new creation. Martin Luther King Jr.'s dreams and hopes were justified, but the reality still seems so far away. The journey is long. The beginning of its fulfillment often seems so small, so humble . . . like Abraham's one son. But God's covenant promises are still valid. God will indeed bring humanity to the fulfillment of the great project. And we are invited to remain faithfully with God on the journey.

14 Starting with Genesis 12.
15 Genesis 12:1-3.
16 Genesis 12:4.
17 Genesis 18:1-15; Hebrews 11:11.
18 Genesis 13, 9-12, 26-33.

For further reflection

1. What can we learn about God in God's revelation to Abraham in Genesis 12? What do we learn, too, about God's *Shalom* project in this part of the Bible?

2. What does the Abraham story teach us about humanity?

3. Abraham's response to God's word is presented all through the Bible as a model of faith. What was included in the concept of "faith" for Abraham? Do I understand "faith" in the same way?

4. Where do I experience the tension between promise and fulfillment in my own life? How do I deal with the tension?

5. After these considerations, what would I like to say to God in prayer?

Dear Monica and Peter,

Well, it looks like Abraham really captured your imagination. Reading between the lines of your letter, I get the impression you are considering what faith is all about. At any rate, the story of Abraham makes it clear that faith is far more than believing something is true, or giving mental assent to theological claims. And it is more than simply "believing in God," or having a vague notion that there is some kind of a God out there. Clearly, "faith" involves being on a journey with God. Faith is opening oneself to God's perspective on life, and then lining up all of life with God's way. Monica, when you write: "Then faith isn't really something that relates just to the religious part of my life, but something that relates to my whole life," you are hitting the nail right on the head. That is exactly what faith is all about.

But in Peter's comments I also detect some critical responses. You are asking how exactly we are supposed to understand God's self-revelation. The story of Abraham makes it seem so simple and clear. God spoke, and Abraham simply heard and understood. But what about today? Does God still speak to people? Can we still hear God? How does God speak in our day? And how can we be sure that what we are hearing is *God's* voice and not just our own imaginations?

You are touching upon a serious problem. It really can happen that we confuse our own imaginations (or the imaginations of others) with God's revelation. But let's not make things more difficult than they really are. When I read your letter and note how carefully you are reading the Old Testament stories, and how you are pondering what they all mean, I am sure that God is speaking to you. I think it is probably one of the mysteries of faith that our certainty grows to the extent that we trustingly and faithfully open ourselves to God and to the great project that God is calling us to join. On one occasion some people asked Jesus to prove that his words really were from God. His answer was, "Whoever is willing to hear these words and put them into practice will be assured that they really are from God" (John 7:17).

Yours truly,
Bernhard

6.
Is everything lost?

God has great plans, but their fulfillment begins with very small steps. This is not the way we like things to be. We want to speed things up. Over and over, Christians have tried to speed up the arrival of God's Kingdom with their own efforts. In fact, some have been so eager, they have even resorted to violence to make things happen. That is the old rebellion against God all over again. It is the old method of Cain and of Lamech.[19] Those who choose such methods have not fully turned their lives back to God. Even Moses is guilty of this. He sees the desperate situation of the Hebrews, the injustices they suffer. He tries to take matters into his own hands. In his attempt to speed up Israel's deliverance, he even resorts to murder. That's when things go terribly wrong.[20] Good simply cannot be reached by evil means. Violent action is not how God's *Shalom* project is brought to its goal. So the Moses story heads off into the wilderness, literally. And the Israelites continue to make bricks for Pharaoh's extravagant building projects. The story heads off in the wrong direction, far away from God's project and God's promise. Or does it?

God is still God

God is still God. What this means is that God's plans, projects, and intentions never change. God did not forget the covenant with Abraham. God stood by old promises and saw the desperate situation that had developed in Egypt. Over and over in the book of Exodus, we read the words, "I will be your God and you will be my people. . . . I have chosen you, though really the whole world belongs to me . . . I am sending you into a new land, so that all nations will be astonished at what they see and will come to know me."[21]

God always stands by the promises God has made. God has chosen a people, and through this people wants to win back all humanity. God's plan is built on peace and justice, not on oppression and violence. God is still God. This means that God takes initiative again and again, a recurring theme throughout Exodus. "I have heard your complaints. I have seen your suffering. I come to your rescue. I will set you free. I will lead you out. I will make you my people. I will give you a land." God takes the initiative. God is the one who acts, who takes the first step, seeking out people, setting them free, and inviting them to be the people of God.

God seeks a project manager

Again God begins with one individual. God's solution is not forced on a collective. And guess whom God starts with now? With Moses, the revolutionary who got it all wrong. With the one who, 40 years previously, tried to accelerate God's plan, forcing it along with a crowbar. God starts again with this man. God says to him: "I am sending you.[22] I will use you to move my project ahead. I am inviting you to be my co-worker." It sounds like the Abraham story all over again. "Get up! Move out!" And again we wait with bated breaths. Can Moses do it? Is Moses willing to take up God's challenge?

The 80-year-old Moses is no longer the young enthusiast

who jumps at the chance. He's become a realist. (Life's experiences tend to do that to people.) God has to fight to get Moses to join the project. In the first place, Moses is not nearly as sure of himself as he once was. "Who? Me?" That's his first reaction to God's invitation. He doubts himself and his abilities. He knows his boundaries this time. Clearly he knows he's no great orator. And God takes his objections seriously. He recruits Moses' brother, Aaron, to speak for him. But that's how God intended humanity to function anyway, not as individuals, not as do-it-yourself-experts, but as people who need the help and the companionship of others.

In the second place, Moses wants to know a little more about who it is that is recruiting him. He needs a name. And God favors him with a revelation of the divine name: "I Am who I Am: I Am the one there for you!"[23] It is a name that makes a huge promise: "I am the One you can always count on. I am the ever-present One. I am the Lord of history, the One who is there, the One who always accompanies you. 'Jahweh' is my Name."

Moses had obviously learned a lot during his 40 years in the desert. The man who would later become the great leader of God's people had learned that he had limitations and needed the help of others. In fact, the crucial conditions for his participation in God's great project were to depend fully on God and to accept the help of his brother. I wonder how many of us will learn these conditions before we turn 80!

Moses is not alone

Here, too, we see that even though God addresses individuals, no person stands there completely isolated and alone. There would have been no Moses for God to call had it not been for his mother, the Hebrew midwives, the daughter of Pharaoh, not to mention Jethro and his daughter Zippora.[24] No one person ever carries the weight of salvation history alone. Men and women who step onto the stage as individuals are always members of a family and a community. What becomes clear in the case of Moses is that God's project is not a male project. God's original creation plan comes into focus here. Man and woman, the ones bearing God's image, are joint participants in God's *Shalom* project

This will also become clear later in Moses' life. What would Moses be without Aaron, Miriam, and Hur? How could he lead the people without the elders and the priests?

God acts

In order for the people of God to come into being, more was needed than a word from God and the human leader Moses. God also needed to act, to intervene concretely in the course of human history. And that is precisely what God did. The way Israel was freed from Egypt is nothing short of a miracle. And Israel never forgot it.[25] Israel's willingness to break free, the Passover event, God's judgment on Egypt, the fact that the slave-owners literally drove their Israelite slaves out of their land—all these are more than mere human achievements.

And then came the great miracle at the Sea of Reeds. The way was blocked in front. From behind the enemies were attacking. And Moses had to reassure a despairing people, speaking to them in God's name: "Don't despair! Wait and watch the Lord rescue you. You can be calm, for it will be God who will fight for you."[26] And that is exactly what happened. The salvation was entirely God's doing. After Israel's journey through the sea, Moses sang with all Israel: "God alone,

Jahweh alone has done it!"[27] And later at Sinai, God was the one who said: "You yourselves experienced how I carried you out as an eagle carries its young; I have brought you safely here to myself."[28] Is it any wonder that Israel's experience of rescue from Egypt showed the pattern of God's acts of salvation on their behalf? Here we see clearly how God's great *Shalom* project is being fulfilled.

Throughout all time, people have found themselves in helpless slavery, over and over again. Humanity without God often resorts to violence, oppression, and injustice. Left to its own resources, humanity is not capable of bringing about peace. Humanity is not capable of overcoming evil, neither the evil on the outside nor the evil within.

Throughout all time, God has proven to be faithful, never giving up on humanity. God who guides history also initiates rescue and salvation. Only God can open a way out of slavery into a new land, a new life. And God is still about the business of inviting. God is inviting people to respond, to join God freely on the journey. God is seeking people who are willing, despite impossible circumstances, to put their full trust in God.

19 Cain murdered his brother (Genesis 4:1-4) and Lamech took revenge 77-fold (Genesis 4:23-24).
20 Exodus 2:11-15.
21 Exodus 3, 6:6-8; 19:5, 6, compared with Deuteronomy 4:1-8.
22 Exodus 3:10ff.
23 Exodus 3:14.
24 Exodus 1-2.
25 Compare texts that look back at Israel's history, for example, Joshua 24:5-8; Nehemiah 9:9-21; Psalm 136:10-20.
26 Exodus 14:13, 14.
27 Exodus 15:3.
28 Exodus 19:4.

For further reflection

1. In what ways can I identify with Moses? In what ways is it difficult to do so? Do I try to force solutions with a crowbar? Do I retreat in resignation? Do I live a comfortable life, far from the afflictions others face? Do I doubt my own abilities? Do I confront God with critical questions? Do I set out to obey, trusting God's help?

2. How do I deal with evil in the world? Is it true that violence cannot be overcome with violence? Can I think of concrete situations to support my view? What does it mean to "Be still and trust God"?

3. If God's name is revealed as "I Am; I Am with you," what does this do to my image of God?

4. Who are the people to whom I am indebted for my very life and being? Who are the people who supply the gifts I do not have and thus supplement what I contribute?

5. If I had the chance, what would I ask Moses about the whole story of Israel's departure from Egypt?

Dear Monica and Peter,

Thank-you for your last letter. The story of Moses and the exodus from Egypt and God's apparently amazing rescue has led to all kinds of tough questions: So was all of this really a miracle, or were there just some remarkable circumstances that fell into place? Was it really only God who made it happen, or did Moses also have a major role to play—or, for that matter, maybe all the Hebrews? And if it really was a major miracle of deliverance, why does God not do that sort of thing anymore? It is certainly not because we have run out of trouble spots, military conflicts, or emergency situations in today's world.

And you expect me to have a satisfactory answer to all these questions ready at hand! Well, it could be that some fortunate historical circumstances contributed to the departure of the Hebrews from Egypt. And certainly, if one sees the whole episode from a larger perspective, one has to credit Moses, Aaron, and others with a major achievement: the oppressed Israelites started to believe that their deliverance was a possibility. If one thinks of the entire process that eventually led to Israel's departure from Egypt, one sees that it did indeed extend over a considerable time period and must have been a complex process. And perhaps in the middle of all of these events, which included many factors hard to identify at the time, people were not necessarily talking about miracles. Yet after Israel was free, and as they began to recount what had happened and to pass on stories to the next generation, one thing was very clear to them: "The fact that we are no longer slaves in Egypt is a miracle from God. The fact that we can now live in freedom—well, we didn't accomplish that. That is something we credit to divine intervention."

Isn't it often like that for us as well? We do our best. We pray. We work at something. We hope and we doubt. Sometimes our efforts are successful, but often we get things wrong. Sometimes circumstances seem to fall into place, and then later seem to work entirely against us. Yet in time we can look back and be sure of one thing: It is a miracle that we made it. Thanks be to God! That is how it often seems to be with miracles. To the neutral observer, they are seldom crystal clear. In fact, even for those who experience them, it is often not all that clear that God was undeniably at work . . . until we look back later on what happened.

The Israelites' deep conviction that God had delivered them from Egypt did give them the strength they needed to move into the future with their God.

Sincerely yours,
Bernhard

7.
Finally!

The time is 1280 years before Christ. Location: a mountainous region in the southern part of the Sinai Peninsula. Overshadowed by the rocky crags of Mt. Horeb, a huge crowd of people have set up camp in the wilderness. There are thousands of them, mostly poor people. Most of them are of Hebrew descent, although there are Egyptians among them as well. Most of them show the telltale marks of long years of slavery. They're mostly families—children crying. Farm animals wander around; household goods surround makeshift and flimsy tent dwellings. A huge crowd of people in the middle of the desert. Is this a people? God's people?

What is the difference between a crowd of individuals and a people group? We know as well as they did: a whole bunch of Christians is not necessarily a Christian fellowship. It is especially important in our individualistic age to pay very close attention to what happened back there in Sinai. And lots had to happen before this bunch of runaway slaves could truly become a people. All the more so if this people group was to become a prototype of God's *Shalom* project. How would God ever turn this bunch of people rescued from Egyptian slavery into a people, into *God's* people? Or, if we ask the question in our day: How will God ever turn this bunch of Christians into a Christian community?

God's *Shalom* Project

Chapters 20-24 of Exodus tell us how *Jahweh* set up a covenant, a legal national constitution, how God invited the people to agree to the terms of the covenant and thus become God's covenant partner. Of course this didn't take place with exactly the same conventions and formalities one would expect in the 21st century. Rather, the process and the people followed the conventions current in that world.

Back then it sounded more like this:

Jahweh is the king

First God's role is defined. "I am *Jahweh*, your God." This is what it says at the top of the covenant document.[29] And then to explain the point more clearly: "Besides me, you are to recognize no other gods." *Jahweh* wants to be king for Israel, king without a rival. In fact God will not allow any other authority to be in competition with God's own. God wants every single individual in this whole crowd to choose God as king and authority, and to choose to live responsible to this authority alone. And since God is a good Lord and king, three incredible promises are immediately pronounced:

1. Your security and freedom are my responsibility: I will go to battle on your behalf.[30]
2. Your daily provisions are my responsibility: I will take care of all your needs.[31]
3. Your journey is my responsibility: I will be your leader.[32]

That's how generous the creator is with the rebels. By showering on them such incredible love, God invites people to become God's people again. The Old Testament calls it election and love; the New Testament calls it grace: undeserved favor. The covenant text continues.

Jahweh wants a "holy people"

God's project remains what it always was—a people freely choosing to live under God's lordship and to carry out a God-assigned role in creation. God does not want a people that seems to worship but in the end does as it pleases. God is seeking a people that is fully on God's side, that aligns all of life the way God directs and leads. God wants a *Shalom* people. God's people are to be transformed into a people completely different from other peoples. God's people are to be a model people, to show how God intended humanity to be. The covenant text speaks of a holy people. That is the role of God's people.

"God is holy," says the text. God is the one unlike all others, unique—not creation but creator, not a rebel but faithful. And God now wants to establish a people, *God's* people, the beginning of a new humanity that is fully on God's side, that belongs to God, that remains true to God, that lines up all of life according to God's will. This will be a holy people.

But the slaves from Egypt don't understand. They can scarcely imagine what it means to be a holy people. How do people live if they decide to turn their lives over to God? What does a life look like that is being lived as God intended? How do people become God's *Shalom* people?

At this point God gives the people another gift. God tells them what a holy life looks like. It can be summarized in two short sentences:

1. Love God with your whole heart.
2. Love your neighbor with your whole heart.

Do you see how God picked up the two age-old questions again? "Where are *you*? Where is *your brother*?" God is not forgetful. When people become people again, people as God intended, then God starts over again with the basics. And what are these? That we recognize God as creator and as the highest authority in life, and that we learn to respect fellow human beings as gifts from God, partners in a common mission.

Of course, the wording is a bit different in the covenant text at Mt. Sinai, but the content is really the same:[33]

1. I am your one God, a God without a rival.
2. Don't try too hard to define me, to put me in a box.
3. Don't try to manipulate me for your own purposes.
4. Don't forget to keep the day of rest.
5. Honor your father and mother.
6. Honor life and don't kill anyone.
7. Don't destroy your marriages.
8. Don't rob anyone of freedom or property.
9. Don't say anything untrue of other people.
10. Be content with what you have; don't covet what other people have.

These "Ten Commandments" sound familiar to us. They, along with the long chapters that follow, are called the Law. And the Law doesn't have a very good reputation. It makes us think of legalism, and that's something we avoid like the plague. But God wants these instructions to be understood very differently. God makes an offer to humanity, to people without God but with a longing for true life. God rescues people from slavery and invites them to live according to God's instructions once more. Doing so means real life, life as God intended for humanity. This is how true harmony and peace become a reality. This is the way to *Shalom*.

Any chance that the Hebrews around Mt. Sinai will accept the invitation? They do. They solemnly participate in a covenant ceremony.[34] The entire text of God's words, the King's decrees, are read aloud, and then carefully taken down in writing. With a loud cry, the people shout out their "Yes!" to the covenant stipulations, and, according to the customs of the time, everything is sealed with an animal sacrifice and the pouring out of blood. God has entered a covenant with a people. People have freely entered this covenant with God and with each other.

And God's way has not changed throughout the centuries. God is still looking for people willing to enter a solemn covenant with God and with one another. Where are the people today who understand themselves to be committed and responsible, not only to God as the highest authority in life, but also to their brothers and sisters? Fellowships like this are signs of peace in a world at war.

29 Exodus 20:2.
30 Exodus 14:13-14. At this point, and again when Israel takes over the land, the question arises: How are we to understand the concept of *Jahweh's* wars (as opposed to Israel's)? The topic would be too large for this book. See the reference to the book by Millard C. Lind in the list of Readings, page 138.
31 Exodus 16.
32 Exodus 13:21.
33 Exodus 20:3-17.
34 Exodus 24.

For further reflection

1. Does the Old Testament law have any meaning for me?

2. What does "the holy life" mean to me?

3. What is my relationship to the church?

4. What does it mean to make God my ultimate authority? Who or what competes with God for that position in my life?

5. Can I connect with the story of God's covenant-making with Israel? What is it that makes this difficult for me?

Dear Monica and Peter,

In this section there were various topics that seem to have disturbed you: What exactly is the holy life? How are we to understand Old Testament laws? Why should we commit ourselves to a congregation? What is the relationship between the reign of God and the authority of human rulers?

I can't deal with all these questions in my letter to you. The last one, however, the one about the authority of the state, does require a few more comments. We are accustomed to relegating religion and faith to the "private, spiritual part" of our lives. Privately, people can believe whatever they want. Publicly, everyone should live according to the "rules" of the society and state. The constitutions of many nations assume this understanding of religion. You may believe whatever you want to believe as long as you also live obediently to the demands of the state.

However, when we read the stories in the Bible (both in the Old Testament and in the New), it is clear that God sees things differently. God's project was not to win over *just* the religious feelings of the Israelite slaves, but their whole beings. God made a claim on the whole person and the whole nation. God wanted to rule over the whole of life. Everything, including ethical behavior, was to be based on God's standards and not on the standards of the rulers of that world. And that is what made

Israel different from other nations of its day. In other nations, priests were involved in dealing with people's "souls," while kings determined what happened in public life. Yet in Israel, God was king; God wanted to rule in both social and political spheres.

This means that biblical faith, right from its foundation onward, is of a unique order. Biblical faith cannot be spiritualized, internalized, and privatized. God wants to be the final authority in all of life—daily life, our workaday world, our social life, our public life. This is why worldly authority must not stand above God's authority—not for biblical Christians. This is why no authority in this world, no boss, no government, no ruler of any kind, can ever have more than a relative authority. This is something Christians and churches of our day have often forgotten.

Consider carefully the impact of recognizing God as Lord of all of life. It means being very discerning about other authorities that try to claim our allegiance. When we get to the New Testament, we come back to this theme again.

'Til next time,
Bernhard

8.
It is a long journey

In daily life we often find ourselves signing contracts and entering alliances. And we join in more major events like entering the covenant of marriage, signing important business agreements, and marking major international treaties with solemn ceremonies. In fact, we are part of countless other agreements—responsibilities, rights, and promises, signed or unsigned, carefully formulated or not. Living together means living in covenant with people. It is one thing to close an agreement, sign a contract, make a promise. It is quite another thing to be faithful, to keep an agreement, to fulfill a promise. If we could be faithful to God and to each other, God's great *Shalom* project would move more quickly toward completion. Why is faithfulness such a difficult thing?

Deep-seated patterns of behavior live on

We saw what happened to thousands of liberated Hebrew slaves more than 3000 years ago in the Sinai desert. God called them into a binding fellowship, a peoplehood under God's own ruling authority. Everyone agreed to the text of the covenant. Everyone joined in the ceremonies and celebrations. That was the easy part. The hard part followed. Would this new people group remain faithful to the covenant? The challenge was great.

If you imagine that people change completely overnight, just because they have entered into an agreement, well, you're in for a rude awakening. Old behavior patterns are not that easily shaken off . . . not then, not now. But God's name is still "I Am; I Am there!" God is on a journey with us, and God has made provisions for the challenges of the journey.

Meeting place: the tabernacle

God instructed Israel to build a "tabernacle" in the desert, a place where God would be present among them. The Hebrew word that we typically translate as "tabernacle" in English should actually be translated "tent of meeting" or "dwelling place." This movable tent became the center of all that God did for Israel during their journey through the desert.[35]

In the first place, God wanted to be very close to the people. Though both invisible and holy, God was, and is, also ever present. And so God instructed the people to build a tent so that God could live among them, identifying fully with them. Our God is a God who sets up a tent in the middle of humanity in order to join us on our journey through life. And when God's people pick up stakes and move on, God and the "tent of meeting" move along with them. God is a "camping" God, a dynamic God, an "I Am there" God.

In the second place, God wanted to schedule regular meetings with Israel. That's why the tabernacle was called a "tent of *meeting.*" Gatherings were regularly scheduled there.[36] Today we call such gatherings "worship services," but this expression is easily misunderstood, as though gathering for one or two hours a week for *worship* constitutes *serving* God for the week. For us, these "worship services" take place in "*holy* sanctuaries." In such places we do "*holy* ceremonies" led by "*holy* people." It all sounds very religious, but it is not very biblical.

For Israel, all of life was holy—not just a few hours a week. And the whole people of God was a holy people, not just the priests. Every event and transaction in life was to be holy, not just certain religious rituals. In fact, what really mattered to *Jahweh*, and what the early meetings with *Jahweh* were all about, was the holiness of *everyday* life. Four main features characterized these meetings, and each one is directed to a specific problem that God's people faced, and indeed, continue to face today.

First of all is the problem of **forgetting**.[37] How quickly humans forget. Memories of the great exodus miracle faded. The covenant obligations were forgotten. So also God's protection and provision in the wilderness.

When the people who experienced all these passed from the scene, how would the memory be kept alive in the next generation? And how would God's great project be brought to completion if people no longer remembered the beginnings, the time of birth, liberation from Egypt, and the covenant ceremonies? This was why God's people, whenever they met, continued to tell the story. This was why people needed, and still need, to continue hearing the story, from generation to generation, from birth to the grave. Numerous Psalms bear witness to the fact that in Israel's "worship services" the story was told and sung, over and over again.

Second, is the problem of **failure**. It is not possible to continue telling the story, honestly and openly, without recognizing anew one's own failures, one's own unfaithfulness.[38] Where has *Shalom* gone? Why can't I look God in the eye like I once did? When we meet with God we can't silence these thoughts, hide this reality. King David and other psalmists knew what misery it brings when we repress the truth, hiding our failures and sins.[39] But what happens when we confess these and speak openly with God about them? How can *Shalom* be restored again?

If we stick with its legal aspects alone, the price of *Shalom* is very high. According to the covenant agreement, God has every right to punish the covenant-breaker. In fact, according to ancient Near-Eastern customs, covenant-breaking was a capital offense. The death penalty applied. But here again, God made an offer of love to the rebels. Those who confessed their failures and sins before God were allowed to lay their guilt symbolically on an animal. This animal then became a vicarious sacrifice. The animal faced the death penalty.[40] *Jahweh* offered the people forgiveness for their sin. And this is why David could pray as he did: "So I decided to confess my sin to you . . . and you, you forgave me everything."[41] God's people can breathe again . . . can live again . . . can look God in the eye again. *Shalom* is once again made possible.

Third, is the problem of **indecision**. We saw earlier that the ability to make decisions is essential to being a human being. In fact humans *must* make decisions. Life consists of one decision after another. One decision is never enough for a lifetime. The decision to make a covenant is one decision. But the decision to keep it is one that has to be made every day.

Every day becomes another opportunity to be faithful or unfaithful. Often we try very hard to avoid decisions like this. We live indecisively, limping along not quite sure where we are heading. And that is precisely why Israel's leaders called the people over and over again to make decisions. Moses, Joshua, Samuel, Elijah—they all confronted the gathered Israelites with the same question: "Whom will you serve? Choose this day! Let us renew our covenant with *Jahweh*!"[42]

God's *Shalom* Project

We, like Israel, cannot rest on previous decisions. We cannot be content with the decisions of our parents and grandparents. We are called over and over again to make our own decisions for or against God.

And finally, there is the problem of **worry and fear**. Israel was often a people of little faith. Understandably so. It took a lot of faith to be God's "holy" people. Questions undoubtedly arose in Israel's mind: Will God protect us if we do not depend on military forces? Will God be our leader if we do not have a human king? Will God bless our fields and crops if we don't practice fertility rituals? Will God supply our daily needs if we share our resources with those who are hungry?

In every age, only those who trust God can live up to their calling as God's "holy" people. Those who constantly fear and worry become self-centered and petty, trying to keep a close eye on their possessions. *Jahweh* knows that. That is why *Jahweh* never tires of renewing promises in the gathered assembly, promises of loving-kindness, daily care, faithfulness, and blessing. God's people need to hear these promises over and over again:

The Lord bless you and keep you.
The Lord make his face to shine upon you,
and be gracious to you.
The Lord life up his countenance upon you,
and give you *Shalom*.[43]

---

35 See Exodus 25-29 for texts that describe the "Tent of Meeting" and the worship there.
36 Exodus 29:42-46.
37 Especially Deuteronomy 8.
38 See Nehemiah 9.
39 For example, Psalm 32:3-4.
40 Leviticus 4, 5, 16.
41 Psalm 32:5.
42 Joshua 24; 1 Kings 18:20ff.
43 Numbers 6:24-26.

For further reflection

1. What do I notice when I compare my understanding of "worship service" with the Old Testament understanding? Are there points of agreement? Are there differences?

2. Do I experience the problem of forgetfulness? What do I do to keep alive the memory of God's great deeds in my life and beyond it? What value do I place on praise and thankfulness in my life?

3. How do I deal with failure and sin in my life? Do I regularly practice confession? Do I find it difficult to admit my failings?

4. Are there times in my life when I renew my covenant and my dedication to God? Is it difficult for me to do this decisively?

5. Do I hear God's promises? Do I truly believe that God will take care of me?

6. What would I like to say to God in prayer after reading this chapter?

Dear Monica and Peter,

Good for you for discussing the topic of "worship service" with others in the congregation, and for thus opening a significant discussion concerning both the form and the content of your worship services. The fact is that our worship services are very often an escape from real life, an escape into a spiritual experience that has very little to do with daily living, rather than (as it should be) an equipping for the realities of life. If you are now trying to find ways of connecting Sunday worship services with normal life throughout the week, congratulations! Keep working at it!

You are asking me how this might look, concretely. I suggest you begin by simply following up on the suggestions made in this chapter. You could begin with questions like this:

1. Do we have a place in our worship services where we simply tell the stories of God's great deeds? That can be a Bible story, or a story from church history, or from the church of today. It can be a story from the life of someone in the congregation. And then the congregation can respond with words or with songs of praise.

2. Do we have a place in our worship services for reconciliation with God? Do we ever talk about sin? About falling short of God's ideal? Do we have a place for confession of sin? Is forgiveness offered and pronounced?

3. Do we have a place in our worship services for renewing covenant? Is there a place where individuals

are called to decision? Are we challenged to commit ourselves anew to God and to our fellow Christians?

4. Is there a place in our worship services for words of promise? Do we hear that God is for us and accompanies us through life?

Of course not everything that belongs to "worship service" has been mentioned here. Meetings with God, both in the Old Testament and in the New Testament, also became occasions where questions from daily life were brought to God. God's people brought their questions and their concerns to God and God gave directions for dealing with them. Do we have a place for this in our worship services? If so, then we can also be sent from worship services into the rest of life, equipped by what we experienced together to represent God faithfully beyond the gathered community. God wants to send us out into the diverse assignments we face in life, newly equipped to be faithful witnesses. Where and how do we experience this as a central aspect of our worship services?

May I encourage you to think deeply about both the content and the form of your worship services. This can lead to a new beginning, both for your gatherings and for your own lives. It can result in worship renewal, but also in changed lives.

I'm looking forward to hearing what comes out of your discussions.

Sincerely,
Bernhard

9.
When things are going well . . .

Back in the 18th century, the English revivalist preacher, John Wesley, wrote: "I fear that wherever wealth increases, serious interest in religion decreases by the same measure. Wherever wealth increases, pride and love for the world and its passions increase in all their varied forms."

Was Wesley correct in his assessment? While this certainly would not apply to every individual wealthy person, it does indeed correspond to what we often observe. Prosperity usually does not agree with people. So why does God's *Shalom* project include a land flowing with milk and honey, to which God will lead Israel? Why does it include overflowing blessing?

Too much milk and honey?

In God's project, the term "land" has multiple meanings. "Land" stands for salvation. It stands for life, for freedom, for peace. God created "land" as the place where people can live and develop. So it is a blessing, a gift from God. But for Israel, "land" also carried with it a mandate. Land did not belong to the people; it belonged to God. So when God's people entered the land, they again took up their role as God's trustees and stewards. This was how God planned it from the beginning. This was why land was not to be exploited.

The land was to be allowed to rest during the Sabbath year. Animals, too, as part of God's creation, were not to be exploited; they also were entitled to a Sabbath rest.

Land was never to become an instrument of social injustice. Nobody was to accumulate property, and nobody was to become impoverished. Every 50 years a Jubilee was to be called in order to re-balance land ownership.[44] It was thus part of Israel's *calling* and *mission* to live in the Promised Land.

Israel was to live in the land in the sight of other peoples, but to live there according to God's instructions. Other nations would see and be amazed . . . and would be drawn to the God of Israel.[45] This is the goal of God's *Shalom* project: a people who has returned to God and through whom God can reach all humanity.

Yet God knew of the danger that Wesley spoke of many centuries later. This is precisely why Moses had to make both the mission and the danger perfectly clear to Israel before the people entered into the Promised Land. "*Jahweh* is bringing you into a beautiful and fertile land. You will have plenty to eat, but do not forget *Jahweh*, your God! Do not ignore God's instructions, laws, and decrees. Do not become proud when all goes well and your possessions increase. Do not forget *Jahweh*, your God. Don't ever think to yourself: 'My own power and the strength of my hands have produced this wealth for me.'"[46]

The warning was clear and to the point, but unfortunately it did not help very much. Israel did not deal well with its prosperity. When everything went well, things started going bad. Two hundred years after the people entered the land, most of the land belonged to a rich upper crust of Israelite society that oppressed the impoverished majority. As far as we know, the Jubilee was never practiced. Lawlessness, corruption, and godlessness were rampant. How could things turn out this way?

What went wrong?

What went wrong was the birth of a small but very dangerous wish that we encounter in the first book of Samuel: Israel wanted to be like the surrounding peoples.[47] Samuel recognized the danger at once and refused to agree. Then *Jahweh* joined in and reacted strongly: "They have rejected me as their king."[48]

Do we see just as clearly what went wrong? God had a project. God was looking for people ready to begin again, ready to become God's people once more. God redeemed a people, made a covenant with them, solemnly celebrated with them an agreement that God would be Israel's king, and Israel God's "holy" (set-apart) people. Israel would *not* live as other nations did. Rather, Israel would be a model of God's *Shalom*, a divine demonstration in this world.

The world was supposed to be able to see the difference. God's people were to live together in such a way that people could see an example of what God originally intended for humanity. They would live a life of peace and justice. Their lives would be characterized by love for God and love for each other. And then the little wish was born: *"We want to be just like other nations!"*

What a slap in God's face. This was like declaring the previous agreement null and void. This was breaking covenant. This was abandoning the mission. The "other nations" were those nations that were living without God, the ones who were still living in rebellion against God. This was the rest of humanity, the part of humanity that ran from God and never returned. Israel's calling was precisely to be different than these. What went wrong? This tiny wish to be *just like all the others*. Everything that followed was the consequence of that.

Israel wanted a king, *like all the others*. Israel began to depend on its military, *like all the others*. Israel began to trust in the fertility cults for its prosperity, *like all the others*. Israel built a magnificent temple, *like all the others*. In Israel there was a rich and powerful elite and an oppressed, poverty-stricken lower class, *as in all the other nations*. Israel was a religious people, but their religion had nothing to do with ethical behavior in daily life, *as in all the other nations*. Israel's kings were rich and mighty, built magnificent castles, and entered treaties with foreigners, *as in all the other nations*. And so, slowly but surely, Israel ceased to be a "holy" nation . . . and slowly but surely became *like all the other nations*. Didn't anyone see what was happening? Didn't anyone sound the alarm? And where was God? Did God just let it all happen?

Those who speak for God

No, God didn't sit idly by. In the deteriorating situation God called men and women who were willing to swim upstream. They were the ones who cried out in the wilderness. They were preachers with uncomfortable messages. They were experienced by the ruling classes as bothersome spoilsports. The Bible calls them prophets. They tirelessly denounced the deteriorating condition of Israel. They courageously preached against the accumulation of wealth and the injustice and oppression that went with it, against the confidence Israel put in its army and its alliances with other nations, against the fertility cults and the empty temple religions. Among them were Elijah, Amos, Hosea, Jeremiah, and others; God's spokespersons, calling Israel back to its senses and to its God. Their message was: "Repent!" Or to translate it more literally: "Turn around! Turn back to the covenant with God!"

Their main concern was the restoration of right relationships, the renewal of *Shalom*. And that included all of the dimensions of *Shalom*—a right relationship to God, just and reconciled relationships with people, even a healthy relationship with God's whole creation. Conversion means all of that, never less than that.

It is not enough to be religious

The prophets, speaking for God, got to the very heart of the matter: There were lots of religious people, but they were not interested in pursuing God's project. And so the prophetic critique was often directed at the religious services, indeed at the whole practice of religion. At the worship centers in Bethel, Amos pronounced in God's name:

I hate, I despise your festivals, and I take no delight in your solemn assembles. Even though you offer me your burnt offerings and grain offerings, I will not accept them; and the offerings of well-being of your fatted animals I will not look upon. Take away from me the noise of your songs; I will not listen to the melody of your harps. But let justice roll down like waters, and righteousness like an everflowing stream.[49]

Hosea said it crisp and clear:

For I desire steadfast love and not sacrifice, the knowledge of God rather than burnt offerings.[50]

Later, Jeremiah stands at the temple gate in Jerusalem and preaches:

Amend your ways and your doings, and let me dwell with you in this place. Do not trust in these deceptive words: "This is the temple of the LORD, the temple of the LORD, the temple of the LORD." For if you truly amend your ways and your doings, if you truly act justly one with another, if you do not oppress the alien, the orphan, and the widow, or shed innocent blood in this place, and if you do not go after other gods to your own hurt, then I will dwell with you in this place, in the land that I gave of old to your ancestors forever and ever.[51]

And Isaiah makes the same point:

"What to me is the multitude of your sacrifices?" says the LORD; "I have had enough of burnt offerings of rams and the fat of fed beasts; I do not delight in the blood of bulls, or of lambs, or of goats. When you come to appear before me, who asked this from your hand? Trample my courts no more; bringing offerings is futile; incense is an abomination to me. New moon and Sabbath and calling of convocation—I cannot endure solemn assemblies with iniquity. Your new moons and your appointed festivals my soul hates; they have become a burden to me, I am weary of bearing them. When you stretch out your hands, I will hide my eyes from you; even though you make many prayers, I will not listen; your hands are full of blood. Wash yourselves; make yourselves clean; remove the evil of your doings from before my eyes; cease to do evil, learn to do good; seek justice, rescue the oppressed, defend the orphan, plead for the widow."[52]

From Amos and Hosea in the 8th century before Christ, right up until Isaiah and Jeremiah in the 6th and 7th centuries before Christ, we hear the same refrain: God detests an inner piety and religious rituals which do not lead to the realization of God's project in daily life. And God's project means justice and *Shalom*. It is not enough to pursue a personal relationship with God and to celebrate beautiful worship services. If these activities do not serve to renew the covenant and to motivate and equip people to participate in God's *Shalom* project, they are just fake religion. They do not lead to the real goal.

And if things don't change . . .

The prophets see other things as well. They see into the future. They do not look ahead merely as predictors, revealing what is up ahead, but rather, they speak as God's mouthpieces, spelling out the shocking consequences that will follow if things go on like this.

In times when everything seemed to be running so smoothly, these prophets were the only ones who saw clearly and spoke out boldly: "If we keep on like this, we are finished!" Unfortunately, their messages usually fell on deaf ears. Sometimes they were arrested and imprisoned. Sometimes they were not allowed to preach. Israel had decided to become like all the other nations. Uncomfortable preachers of repentance were a bother. And so Hosea spoke God's word of judgment, God's bottom line: "You are no longer my people and I am no longer your God!"[53]

In the light of these observations from the Old Testament, shouldn't Christians in the rich and satisfied West be asking some serious questions as well? Is the church still God's demonstration of peace and love in this world? Hasn't the church in every century, again and again, become just like those outside the church? Where are the prophets who are swimming upstream? Where are the voices in the wilderness, courageously willing to be unpopular? Where are the Christians who are establishing visible communities that put into practice God's *Shalom* project?

---

44 See Leviticus 25.
45 Deuteronomy 4:5-8; 28:9-10.
46 Deuteronomy 8:7-20.
47 1 Samuel 8:20.
48 1 Samuel 8:7.
49 Amos 5:21-24.
50 Hosea 6:6.
51 Jeremiah 7:3-7.
52 Isaiah 1:11-17.
53 Hosea 1:9.

For further reflection

1. Why was the temptation to try to be like other nations such a fatal temptation for Israel?

2. Do I see any parallels between Israel's problems and those Christians face today?

3. Where do I experience the tension between fitting in with the "world" and being separate from the "world"? How are Christians called to be "different" today?

4. How was the role of the prophet defined in this chapter?

5. Where are there prophets today? Does God still send us prophets? What would their message be today?

6. After all these considerations, what would I like to say to God in prayer?

Dear Monica and Peter,

It seems as though my question about the parallels between ancient Israel and the situation today gave you lots to talk about. Especially you, Monica (since you grew up in a rather conservative Christian environment), seem to struggle with the idea that Christians are supposed to be different from other peoples and cultures. You write that during your childhood and youth you were bombarded with statements like: Christians don't do this; Christians don't do that; Christians are supposed to be different from the world. You obviously experienced this idea of Christianity as backward, legalistic, and offensive—certainly not as an inviting alternative to the secular life of contemporary society.

I promise you that I won't waste any ink trying to persuade you to accept that kind of stagnant segregation from the world, the kind you reject from your youth. God's *Shalom* project has a completely different goal than that. As Christians we are invited to live in such a way that we are a sign of the future world already breaking into this world. God's people are challenged to take their place among the great pioneers, those who point the way for others, in terms of reconciliation and peace, honesty and justice, faithfulness and commitment.

In a world that is looking for models, examples, and pilot projects in all areas of human society, it is precisely this future-oriented aspect of Christian living that is so desperately needed. That is why I join you, Peter, in seeing lots of parallels between the period of the monarchy in ancient Israel and the church in our day. Unfortunately, Christian churches today are far too often indistinguishable from the surrounding society, and far from the alternative society envisioned in Scripture.

You ask me if there are prophets around today. I'm not convinced that the true prophets today are always the ones who claim the gift of prophecy. What I can say is that you yourselves—if you hold to what you are discovering, put it into practice in your own lives, and speak up when the time is right—will be speaking and acting prophetically in your own situation. Of course, you are not to make it your goal to become prophets. Just live wholeheartedly as God's co-workers and everything else will follow in its proper time.

Shalom,
Bernhard

10.
. . . and when they are not!

Brand new parents . . . their baby boy is born. He is an only child. With love and dedication they raise him. The first years are wonderful. The little boy sits on Mom's lap; learns to walk holding Dad's hand. The boy grows bigger, older, and also more independent. He reaches the age of puberty and things start to get more difficult. He doesn't listen to his parents anymore. One day he storms out of the house; he has no plans to return. It's not a healthy detachment from his parental home. Rather he's on the road, heading for disaster. His parents invite him back, tears filling their eyes. But it is no use. They are torn up inside as they observe their son. But there is nothing they can do. He's now of age. He's making his own decisions. He'll live as he chooses and will have to deal with the consequences of his choices.

Using this illustration, all too common in real human life, God describes what happens to the people of God. The story is recorded for us by the prophet Hosea.[54]

Once more God had to pay the price for the way God created humanity. Humans were created with the ability to decide. Would theirs be a decision to be God's co-workers? Or would it be a decision to live an independent life, unconcerned about God's plan? Once more the second choice was made. And as always, there were consequences. Israel got exactly what it chose.

Plaything of the nations

Israel decided to let human kings be its leaders. Israel wanted to entrust its national security to its army, wanted to secure its political future by means of political treaties, wanted to secure its prosperity by participating in the fertility cults. Israel was allowed to make its choices. But nothing good came of them. In the 8th century B.C.E., the Assyrians wiped out the northern part of Israel. King Pekah was of no help. Neither was a treaty with Syria, nor Israel's army, nor calling on Baal.

The smaller southern kingdom around Jerusalem survived another 120 years, though the credit should go mostly to the political circumstances of the Near East, not to Israel's own strength as a nation. And then around the turn of the century, from the 7th to the 6th B.C.E., time ran out for Jerusalem as well. Their little army was of no help. Neither did it help to run for shelter into the arms of the Egyptians. And a false trust in the "Temple of the Lord" was of no use either.

Israel wanted to live life without God. And that is what Israel got to do. Instead of experiencing the freedom Israel had been promised, Israel went back into bondage—not as slaves in Egypt this time, but as captives to the Babylonians. Instead of experiencing the promises of peoplehood, a remnant of scattered and deported persons was all that was left. Instead of dwelling in the Promised Land, Israel sat beside the "waters of Babylon" and wept.[55]

Once more it became shockingly obvious: Humanity preferred to master life without God. And once more, anxious questions need to be asked: Is this finally the end of God's project? Will God ever find any who will remain faithful? Will God even give humanity another chance?

If God were human

According to human standards and rights, the story of God and humanity should have been over long ago. The punishment for breaking the covenant was the death penalty. Old Testament law permitted a father to take a rebellious son to court and to have him sentenced with the death penalty.[56] But God is not like that. God announced through the prophet Hosea: "How could I ever give you up? . . . How could I ever leave you in the lurch? . . . I cannot destroy you. Even the thought of it tears me up. My compassion is aroused. I will not carry out my fierce anger, for I am God and not a mere human. I, the holy God, am coming to help you, never to destroy you."[57] This is what God is like. This is the Gospel— the good news! God never gives up on humanity. True, we have to carry the consequences of our wrong decisions, and these can be bitter at times. Those who make their bed will have to lie in it. And yet it's true both for the individual and for humanity as a whole: God never gives up on us.

The next chapter in God's project

Israel had taken a terrible beating, but there was still a small faithful remnant. We only know a few names: Daniel, Ezekiel, Esther, Nehemiah, Ezra, a few others. God saw them. God faithfully accompanied them through their dark years of exile. And in the darkest hours, God gave them a vision and new hope. And so a new chapter in God's *Shalom* project began.

With their inner eyes, the prophets of the exile saw this new vision: A day was coming, when God would intervene once more. In that day, God's reign would be all-embracing, would break through in all its fullness. Old dreams would finally come true. Peace and justice would break through. It would be a day of judgment over everything godless and evil and simultaneously a day of salvation for all who are faithful. The present may still look dark, but the future belongs to *Jahweh*.

This new future era would be totally different, for God would intervene once more. Ezekiel prophesied: God will pour out the Holy Spirit, and the people of God will be fully renewed. Past guilt will be wiped away, and the renewed people of God will live faithfully according to God's will.[58] Jeremiah received glimpses of the same thing and announced that God would make a new covenant. This new covenant would be written on people's hearts, and again a people would come into existence who lives according to God's will.[59]

Isaiah saw most clearly that all these new things would depend on the arrival of God's "Sent One." God would again begin with an individual, one who would be faithful to God. Isaiah called this one the "Servant of the Lord." He would bring justice and peace to this world. He would be the *Shalom* bringer for all humanity. He would reconcile rebellious humanity back to God. He would pay the *Shalom* price, so that *Shalom* would be restored between God and humanity. He would live as a model for others, live as God intended humans to live.[60]

Ever since those days in exile, the remnant of Israel has lived with this hope. And Israel's history, from those days onward, has been marked by the burning question: When? When will God intervene? How will God do it? How long do we still have to wait? When will the "Sent One" ever arrive? And how will we recognize him?

God's *Shalom* Project

As New Testament Christians, we believe that Jesus is the promised "*Shalom* bringer." With Jesus, the promised new age of salvation began. And yet, both as individuals and as churches, we still at times experience something very similar to what Israel experienced: When we have hit the bottom, when our self-chosen paths clearly lead us away from God and head us for destruction, then we find ourselves listening once again for God's voice, and hearing it. And when we do, we can claim the same promise that comforted and challenged Israel: God never gives up on us. New beginnings are always possible.

54 Hosea 11:1-6.
55 Psalm 137.
56 Deuteronomy 21:18-21.
57 Hosea 11:8, 9.
58 Ezekiel 36:23-27.
59 Jeremiah 31:31-40.
60 Texts from Isaiah 40-55.

For further reflection

1. Examine the text from Hosea 11 once more and then ask: What needs to change about my image of God?

2. Have I ever personally experienced, or has my congregation experienced, what it means to hit the bottom? What does the experience of Old Testament Israel have to teach me/us in such situations?

3. What role do prophets play in tough times? Do we need these kinds of prophets today?

4. When I look back at the various periods in Old Testament history—deliverance from Egypt, the time of the monarchy, exile in Babylon—which of these periods is most like what we are experiencing today?

5. As I have worked my way through the Old Testament, what have I learned? And what has been happening to me in the process?

6. After this study of the Old Testament, what would I like to say to God in prayer?

Dear Monica and Peter,

We have completed our journey through the first part of the Bible. Thanks for your summary comments on the Old Testament. I see three themes coming through clearly in your letter:

1. The God of the Old Testament is not a mysterious, violent, and incomprehensible God, but rather a God of love, attentive to human need. Of course there are still some texts in the Old Testament that continue to mystify us. But what comes through clearly is a picture of a God who is amazingly faithful, who journeys with us, and who never gives up on us, even in (or especially in) our darkest hours.

2. You have correctly noted that the Old Testament does not portray a legalistic religion that does not yet know of God's grace. On the contrary, the Old Testament message is one of God's undeserved love and mercy toward humanity. The Old Testament is Gospel: Good News.

3. You correctly observed that already in the Old Testament, God is concerned with all of humanity, and that God chose a people, that they might be sent into the world to become a blessing for all peoples. That means that the Old Testament already has a missionary focus.

I also note that you still have some serious questions, that you point out some very serious problems that still need solutions: (1) How are we supposed to understand war in the Old Testament? (2) Why did God choose Israel and not some other nation? What about all those other nations? (3) To what extent is it even possible to look at Old Testament history and apply its lessons to our own day? (4) What is the major difference between the testaments? What actually changed with the coming of Jesus Christ?

To try to answer all of these questions would not be possible in a book of this length, let alone in this letter. But some of these questions will be dealt with very directly in the chapters that follow.

That said, I'll be back in contact later . . . in the New Testament.

Bernhard

11.
Jesus, ben Joseph from Nazareth

Setting our hopes on the Messiah

The wheels of history move along. We're now looking at a period about 2000 years ago. Rome is the ruling power in the known world around the Mediterranean Sea, including the Middle East, where most of the events connected with God's *Shalom* project have been taking place.

In the first century, the surviving remnant of God's people was living under foreign occupation, far from the promised *Shalom*. Within Israel there were various ways of dealing with foreign rulers. The rich upper class had come to terms with the occupying power. The poor people living in Galilee groaned under the burden of heavy taxation. Some of them had organized themselves into revolutionary groups whose goal was to shake off by force the foreign rulers. Still others retreated into the desert to wait in pious seclusion for God's intervention. But most Israelites were, in one way or another, setting their hopes on the promised Messiah, the one who would come to defeat the Romans and restore God's people to nationhood once more. That is how they imagined God's *Shalom* project would move ahead.

A man from Nazareth

At this time a man arrived on a scene who created a sensation: Jesus, ben Joseph from Nazareth. His home was the poverty-stricken region of Galilee in northern Palestine. His father was a craftsman in the small village of Nazareth. Jesus himself probably also learned his father's profession. There would have been nothing special to notice in the life of this man had not his life taken a surprising turn, somewhere around his thirtieth birthday. There was a movement of repentance started by someone named John, and, along with many other God-fearing Jews of his day, Jesus joined the movement. He was baptized by John in the Jordan River. And that is where it happened.

Jesus heard a voice from heaven while being baptized. And the voice made it clear to him: He was the promised Messiah. But his Messianic "rule" would not take the form of a mighty kingship; rather he would be the Servant of God, the *Shalom* bringer predicted by Isaiah.[61] Alone in the desert Jesus struggled many days with this calling. What did it mean for him to be the Messiah in the form of a servant, so that he could bring God's *Shalom* to humanity?

Just as with the first humans, Adam and Eve, so also Jesus had to make the crucial decision. Would he choose of his own free will to place his life under the Lordship of God, or would he opt for his own autonomy? And as with Adam and Eve, so also now the voice of evil whispered in his ear. After nearly six weeks, he had made his basic decision, a sensational decision. Here was a human who did not opt for autonomy but chose a life of full obedience to God. Later Jesus would say, "My food is to do the will of the one who sent me."[62] His life from then on would not be determined by human wishes, but by God's will. Did God finally find the fully faithful human? Did this breathe new life into God's project once more? Would Jesus' good intentions be sustained?

Is this the Messiah?

Having made the basic decision in the depths of his heart, Jesus returned from the wilderness and started to preach: "The great event you have all been waiting for has arrived: God's rule is being established!"[63] The people listened eagerly. And the big questions were these: What happens next? What will God do? Will the holy war against Rome begin and Israel be restored to national prominence?

No, Jesus had a different message. Rather, Jesus traveled throughout the countryside and spread the invitation: "Believe that God's rule is coming to reality. Change your minds and your lives. Set aside your selfish lifestyles and turn your lives fully to God."[64]

In Nazareth, his hometown, he announced the arrival of the Jubilee, the *Shalom* order which the prophets had predicted would characterize the messianic age.[65] Was anyone really listening? The people were skeptical. "Is this really the promised Messiah?" they asked. If he was, then a new chapter in God's *Shalom* project was beginning. It was time to get on board. This would be something too great to miss. But what if he were a false prophet? What if he were a fanatic? An impostor?

That which began in Galilee spread like wildfire throughout the whole land. This Jesus, son of Joseph the carpenter—could he ever stir up people's imaginations! He claimed to be one sent by God, the Father, in heaven. He announced the arrival of a new era of salvation and invited people to follow him. In God's power he healed the sick, drove out demons, and forgave sinners. He fed the hungry, sat down with tax collectors and prostitutes. He preached boldly against false piety and injustice. And instead of setting off war against Rome, he preached and lived a life of love for enemies. Instead of restoring national Israel, he invited people to freely choose a way of life that modeled God's *Shalom* order. And those who responded became a visible sign of God's new social order.[66] Jesus began by gathering around himself a small community of men and women, his followers. He taught them the secrets of God's *Shalom* Kingdom. They were to begin living their lives according to the way God intended, according to the way of God's *Shalom* project: reconciled to God, to fellow human beings, to creation itself. When they did this, they would become visible signs and clear examples to the rest of humanity. When others observed the Jesus community, many would join, giving up rebellion against God and beginning a new life in the restored community. And in this way God's *Shalom* would be experienced once more.[67]

Jesus' new program sounded pretty strange to many people. "Could this be the Messiah?" they wondered. He didn't fit the pattern. He was nothing like the kind of Messiah they had imagined or awaited. Even though he retreated continually for prayer in lonely places, he was no Essene, one who escaped the world and in seclusion awaited God's intervention. Even though he taught like a rabbi, he was certainly no pharisaical scribe for whom the law was more important than people. Even though his preaching was the stuff revolutions are made of, he was no zealot, no weapon-wielding builder of God's Kingdom. Although he accepted the poor and the oppressed, he was no bread-Messiah, one whose focus was on material provisions alone.

Was he really the Messiah? That was the burning question. More and more people were sensing that he truly was. And if he really was, then he represented the way to God; then he himself was the truth; then he was the embodiment of real life.[68] Then everything centered around him. But what if he was merely a false prophet?

Wherever Jesus went, people were divided. Many, especially from the lower classes, became his followers. Many were skeptical and disillusioned. The pious ones didn't think he was pious enough. The freedom fighters didn't think he fought enough. He posed a threat to the status of the religious leaders. Those who controlled the temple were no longer willing to stand by and watch a wandering preacher from Galilee strut around as a Messiah and deceive the people. And so pressure was put on the Romans. This man had to go. He was a revolutionary. And he was finally executed as a political criminal.[69]

Even in his last hours, when his closest companions tried to persuade him to resort to violence and his enemies provoked him, he remained faithful to his highest principles: "Your will, Father, not mine, be done."[70]

And God's will was and is the way of love, not the way of violence.[71] So it came about that Jesus of Nazareth, the truly faithful one, the true human, the Servant of God, was brutally executed. A sad story. Does that mean that God's final opportunity to win back humanity was wiped out? Did godlessness win a final victory?

He is the Messiah!

On the third day after Jesus' death, the rumors started to spread: "He's alive! Jesus of Nazareth has been resurrected from the dead." Of course it would have remained just a rumor, one that people would quickly forget, if it were not for Jesus' followers. They insisted that they had seen the risen

Jesus. He had eaten with them. He had spoken with them. Now they were absolutely certain: He is truly alive again! He is indeed the promised Messiah. They had all been terrified and disillusioned, sitting together behind locked doors. Suddenly Jesus came walking right through the closed doors and addressed them: "*Shalom* be with you!"[72] And then he had sent them out to take his place, announcing to people everywhere that God's *Shalom* Kingdom was being established, gathering together into God's new *Shalom* community all those who would listen.[73] And so began a new era in God's *Shalom* project.

---

61 The voice of God from heaven (Matthew 3:17 and parallels) contains a remarkable combination of three Old Testament texts: a "Messiah-king" announcement from Psalm 2:7, an announcement of the Servant of God from Isaiah 42, and an allusion to Abraham's "beloved son," destined to be killed, out of Genesis 22:2.
62 John 4:34.
63 Matthew 4:17, par.
64 Mark 1:14,15, par.
65 Luke 4:16ff; Isaiah 61:1ff.
66 This is what the Sermon on the Mount, Matthew 5-7, is all about.
67 Matthew 5:13-16; John 13:34, 35; 17:21.
68 John 14:6.
69 For example, John 9:16; 10:19-21; 11:45-57; 18:1-19, 30.
70 Mark 14:36, par.
71 Matthew 26:36-56; 27:39-44.
72 John 20:19.
73 Matthew 28:18-20; John 20:21-23.

For further reflection

1. What do I imagine the earthly Jesus was really like? And what does the life of Jesus mean to me?

2. How did I react to the presentation of Jesus in this chapter? On what points did I agree and where did I question or disagree with what I read?

3. Can I put myself in the situation of the people who lived around Jesus in the first century? How would I have responded to this Jesus of Nazareth?

4. Reflecting again on the temptations of Jesus: In what way were these real temptations for Jesus? Am I ever tempted in similar ways?

5. Do I consider myself a follower of Jesus as this is described in the Gospels? How does this express itself concretely in my life? Reading once more the Sermon on the Mount (Matthew 5-7) do I accept this as a standard for my life of discipleship?

6. Do I understand and experience the church as the fellowship of Jesus, people living together as the people of God according to the standards of the Sermon on the Mount?

Dear Monica and Peter,

Clearly you were a bit shocked by the way I presented Jesus. You claim that what I wrote made Jesus seem so normal, so human, so earthly. You must have grown up with a very different picture of Jesus. You claim that I didn't even hint at the deity of Jesus. Not only that, but I didn't even refer to Jesus' death as a substitutionary sacrifice.

Well, let's slow down and take one thing at a time. First of all, let me assure you that there is much more to say about Jesus than what I included in this chapter. If you want to hear more about Jesus' death as a substitutionary sacrifice, you will have to wait a while longer. However, I will admit that I quite intentionally presented Jesus in the way I did. So maybe it was a bit one-sided, but there is a reason for that.

Traditionally the church has strongly emphasized that Jesus is the Son of God, that he had supernatural powers, that he forgave sin, and that he himself lived a sinless life. The Gospels make these claims and I accept them. But the Gospels also present Jesus as a human, a man from Nazareth who struggled and doubted, wept and suffered. We are told in the Bible that Jesus was human like we are (Hebrews 2:14-18; 4:15).

This Jesus came into a highly charged political situation, and it was into this situation that he spoke his message. He came with both feet planted firmly on the ground of historical reality. He challenged the religious, economic, and military powers of the day, conflicting with them over real economic and political circumstances in Palestine under Roman rule. Traditionally, this Jesus has been pushed into the background.

That is why I considered it best to begin my presentation of Jesus with a chapter that presents Jesus as fully human. Of course I am aware that any presentation of Jesus raises significant theological issues. How are we to imagine Jesus as both God's Son and also as a human like us? Traditional Christian confessions have attempted to capture this mystery by speaking of the two natures of Jesus. Jesus is simultaneously fully God and fully human. That might be sufficient if its goal is to warn us against going too far to the left or the right. But it certainly does not answer all the questions.

If we want to know what it meant for Jesus to be truly tempted, or to what extent Jesus was omniscient (did he know everything?), the traditional church confessions will not supply the answers. Some of these questions cannot be answered once and for all. Any proposed answer simply raises new questions. So for now I will simply leave you with the somewhat one-sided presentation of Jesus as a human. Let it be for us a reminder that in Jesus God truly did become a man, someone fully human, as we are. In order to come near to us, God actually became one of us. Talk about Good News!

Please remember, we are just beginning our reflections on the person of Jesus Christ. Take your questions with you and move on with the *Shalom* project. Some of the answers will become clearer in the chapters that follow.

I am looking forward to your continued responses to what I'm presenting.

Bernhard

12.
God's dynamite

Left alone

They were sitting there—more than a hundred of them, all men and women who had followed Jesus. Many of them witnessed the awful things Jesus went through, the rejection, the trial, the execution. And most of them also met the resurrected Jesus. And now they were sitting there. Apparently Jesus *had* to go away—to his Father, he had said. And they were supposed to wait. John comments: "He told us before he left that he was sending us, just as the Father had sent him.[74] That sounds as though we are to be his representatives, those who will carry on the work he began. I have a sneaking suspicion we're not quite up for that. Or is there someone here who thinks they might measure up to Jesus?" Silence.

"And then there's the commission to make disciples,"[75] someone else piped up. "How are we to win other people to follow Jesus, when Jesus himself isn't here anymore?" "What troubles me the most," added James, "is Jesus' assignment to go to Samaria and to Rome and to the end of the world.[76] Could he really have meant that? What do we have in common with those unclean people? I for one am not about to make contact with them!" "I'm afraid," said another from the other corner of the room. "Just think of what they did to him. Do you think we'll be treated any differently? If we leave here and speak up for Jesus' cause, we're finished. Didn't Jesus himself once predict that people would hate us on account of him and drag us into court?"[77]

Then Mary Magdalene spoke up. "But don't you remember his other words? Didn't he say he would be with us always, to the end of the age? Didn't he say he would be gone only a short time and then would come back in the Spirit? Didn't he say that the Holy Spirit would be our Advocate and our Helper? Didn't he in fact promise us that after a little while he would fill us with power from above so that we could fulfill our commission? Shouldn't we wait and pray and above all make sure we don't lose heart?"[78]

Dynamite from heaven

It was Pentecost, a feast during which the Israelites brought to God the first fruits of the harvest. That's when it happened. Luke, who later reported the event, used pictures to describe it—a storm wind from heaven—fire from above! That is the symbolic language the Old Testament uses to tell of God's great intervention. God's "fire" came, and suddenly these fearful and distraught disciples were filled with supernatural power and turned into courageous witnesses for Jesus. Once again, God's intervention was visible and audible. People from diverse nations and language groups heard in their own languages and dialects as the disciples spoke of Jesus. It is as though God wanted to show that the confusion of tongues at Babel was finally being reversed. A new era was beginning.[79]

Of course this raised lots of questions. What did it all mean? Was there an explanation? What was happening? It was Peter who explained things: "This is what the prophets were talking about," he began. And he explained that in that very hour the promise that God's Spirit would be poured out in the last days was being fulfilled.

This was undeniable evidence that Jesus truly was the Messiah. This was undeniable evidence that God had truly intervened once more and had begun a new chapter in God's *Shalom* project. This was what all the prophets looked forward to: God would intervene once more; God would forgive the sins of the past; God would make a new covenant; God would fill people with the Holy Spirit; God's people would be reconstituted and be faithful to God and live according to God's commandments. And all that, Peter explained, was now coming to pass through Jesus' life, death, and resurrection, and through the pouring out of God's Spirit. Now God's *Shalom* project was really getting going! It was like the first fruits of another kind of harvest.

The results

What happened when hundreds of people were gripped by Peter's preaching, and when they decided to get involved in God's project? What happened when hundreds of people admitted that they had been rebels against God? What happened when hundreds of people were converted, changed their lives, and began to follow Jesus? What happened when hundreds of people had their sins forgiven and were filled with God's Spirit, with God's power? This is what Luke summarizes in the first pages of the book of Acts.

1. These people became a fellowship, a community, a new "people of God." It is a serious misunderstanding if we think that being Christian is just being a host of redeemed individuals. God has always wanted a *people*. When God intervenes in people's lives through the power of the Holy Spirit, a community, a church, is born.

2. If a community is to come into existence, then God has to work at the lives of individuals. The goal is not only a new relationship with God, but also new relationships with the people around us. Do we still remember the beginning of the biblical story? "Where are you, Adam?" and, "Where is your brother, Cain?" These two age-old questions are always relevant.

The story of the book of Acts is the amazing story of egotistical, self-centered behavior converted into attitudes of sharing and caring, of being ready to let go and to share for the benefit of the whole community. And concrete actions did take place. We read in Acts that no one thought of his/her possessions as something to own privately. Everyone understood material goods as gifts from God, given for the benefit of the whole community. That is why there were no needy people in this community of the Spirit. The very visible expressions of life in this community attracted others, and regularly people expressed interest in joining the community and in working together at God's project. Isn't this exactly what God had always wanted?

3. With an incredible decisiveness and commitment, these early believers learned what it means to truly follow Jesus. They had been given the tremendous assignment of passing on the life and the teaching of Jesus, understanding this to be the standard for people to live by. I wonder how often Peter, Matthew, or James reminded people of Jesus' Sermon on the Mount. Empowered by God's Spirit, these early Christians began to change their very lifestyle, modeling themselves after the example and the teaching of Jesus. Is it any wonder that people observed the community and responded with awe and amazement?

4. Fearlessly, Peter, John, and the others openly testified about their faith to any who would listen. Even when they were opposed by political authorities, they remained committed to the mission of proclaiming Jesus, the Messiah. God's project was such a pressing concern that nobody could keep them silent. And God stood by them, visibly confirming their words with great signs and wonders.

Then and now, these are the things that happen when the power of the Holy Spirit is at work. This is God's dynamite.[80] God energizes the disciples of Jesus with this explosive power, thus moving the great *Shalom* project forward.

Of course the great question must be asked: Who is ready to be open to this power and to let the Spirit of God get to work?

74 John 20:21.
75 Matthew 28:19.
76 Acts 1:8.
77 Matthew 10:17-19; John 15:20.
78 Matthew 28:20; John 14:16; Luke 24:49.
79 Acts 2:1-13.
80 Luke delights in using the Greek word *dunamis*, (= power, might), when speaking of the powerful works of God's Spirit.

For further reflection

1. What actually happened at Pentecost? How would I express the significance of Pentecost in my own words?

2. What role does the Holy Spirit play in my life and in the life of my congregation?

3. What was the impact of the Holy Spirit's work in the early Christians and in the first

churches? Which of these do I experience and which do I not experience in my own life? Which does the church as a whole experience?

4. In which areas of my life would I want God to pour out a greater measure of the power of the Holy Spirit?

5. How would I want God's Spirit to be more active in my congregation?

Dear Monica and Peter,

I sense that you enjoy New Testament themes. They are more familiar to us. And you are right; they seem to apply more directly. Yet sometimes they are so familiar we run the risk of missing what they really want to teach us. What is the significance of Pentecost for our lifestyles and for the committed Christian community? Don't be led astray by those who want to convince you that the form of community practiced in the early church was unique and should not be practiced in our day. Some even argue that the community of goods practiced in the early church was a big mistake and that the church suffered poverty later because of it.

I know that some Bible interpreters, well-known ones at that, often fail to draw the connection between the pouring out of the Holy Spirit and the form of Christian community that emerged as a result of it. But why in the world would Luke have described the common life of the Christian community right after telling us what happened at Pentecost? To show us a bad example? Something we are supposed to avoid? Hardly. Why would he have described the early church with lots of allusions to Old Testament promises that were being fulfilled: the Spirit was poured out; the People of God were being recreated; these people were obeying God's commands once more (e.g. Ezekiel 36:26-28); a new

Jubilee Year was being announced; the lame were now leaping; prisoners were being set free; the poor were being fed (Isaiah 61:1-3; Luke 4:18, 19)? The only possible explanation is that Luke wanted to make perfectly clear that God's Spirit creates a new community.

Now to the sentence in your letter that I found most encouraging: "If everything in this chapter is true, then we have to change lots of things in our church." How true. But don't forget something very important. In the opening chapters of Acts, Luke was not simply presenting a brand new social experiment. It wasn't by chance that Luke highlighted four main emphases in the new fellowship that the Spirit brought into being (Acts 2:42): Holding fast to the word of Jesus as it was passed on by the apostles; a united and mutually committed fellowship of believers; the celebration of Jesus' presence in shared communion; and common prayers. If you practice the same priorities, the church will change indeed. The Spirit of God will make sure of it.

Keep me informed. I am eager to hear how things develop in your fellowship.

Sincerely,
Bernhard

13.
For those who understand this . . .

A puzzled Jewish theologian

Damascus. A man lies blind on a bed. His head is spinning. The events of recent days were turning his life upside down. He was a Jew, a well educated theologian, a conservative member of the Pharisaic party. His Hebrew name was Saul; the Greeks called him Paul. With great commitment and diligence he was opposing the sect of Jesus-followers. That was until recently. Two days ago Jesus himself met him. And now his thoughts are in turmoil. This person, Jesus, son of Joseph of Nazareth—was he really the Messiah? But he was put to death on the cross as an outlaw. Yet his disciples were claiming he rose again.

Paul's mind raced: If that were really true, it would mean that the new age of salvation had dawned. But how could it all fit together? What could it all mean? Why the cross? Why did Jesus have to die? How did this fit with the Old Testament predictions? What was the connection between all this and God's Kingdom, God's project? And what was the meaning of the resurrection? Was there any rhyme or reason to all of this?

What a theological challenge, trying to put all the pieces together. Most of all for Paul, but also for Peter, John, James,

Mark, Matthew, Luke, and others. They were all at work on this assignment. Through the Holy Spirit, God enabled them to find appropriate places for the events surrounding Jesus of Nazareth in the larger picture of God's project. Three of the main conclusions they drew deserve closer inspection.

God became a man

Well, what was God supposed to do with humanity? Humans had turned out to be rebels. Of course God could have given up on the project, left humanity to its fate, its self-destruction. But, no. Rather, God opened a brand new chapter in the great *Shalom* project. It was a daring move: God would physically join humanity. The Father would send the Son. In Jesus of Nazareth the miracle would happen. Those who would see Jesus would see what the Father is like. Those who would hear Jesus' voice would hear the voice of God. In Jesus, God would be present with humanity.

One might call it an ultimate declaration of love, an ultimate invitation extended to humanity. If the God of heaven came down in person, poured out love as only God can, extended the invitation one more time, perhaps humans would respond as they should.[81] And there was more. In the incarnation (God becoming a human) the apostles saw something else. Jesus of Nazareth was also a true human, one who remained faithful to God to the very end. One might say Jesus was a prototype, one who lived as God had always intended humans to live. One might say Jesus was a second Adam. He was the first of a new humanity that does not live in rebellion against God.

The extent of human rebellion against God was clearly displayed in the way people responded to Jesus of Nazareth. The servant of God was murdered. And in this way the godlessness of the world, even of the pious Jewish world, was clearly revealed. The people showed their true colors in the way they treated Jesus. Paul puts it like this: "He [Jesus] made a public spectacle of them."[82] And that of course raises another big question: Why did Jesus have to die?

Jesus died for us

Jesus had to die. Jesus himself had tried to persuade his disciples of that. He said he had come to give his life as a ransom for humans.[83] His death was not an unexpected mishap. It belonged to God's project. Paul heard it explained that way by the other apostles. They were saying: Christ died for our sins as it was already predicted in the Old Testament.[84] But what did this mean?

We know from the Old Testament that the death penalty was prescribed for breaking covenant. And we also learned that the coming day of the Lord was understood as a day of judgment. And we learned that God had no desire to be rid of rebellious humanity; rather, God wanted to save humanity. So what was God to do? The apostles began to interpret Jesus' death as a vicarious judgment on humanity. Isaiah 53:5, 6 was no doubt the text that held the key. There it says of the promised Servant of God, "He was wounded for our transgression . . . upon him was the punishment that made us whole." This was why Paul could say: "One has died for all . . . For our sake God made him to be sin who knew no sin, so that in him we might become the righteousness of God."[85] Because of this, Paul understood the whole "Jesus project" as one of God's great acts of deliverance for humanity.

For us, the Son gave up the glory of the Father in heaven and became a human. For us, he remained true, true to the very end. He invested his whole life for us. For us, he suffered the penalty for covenant-breaking. For us, he made peace and reconciliation with God possible. Jesus is the *Shalom* bringer, the one who creates peace between God and rebellious humanity. This insight became the overriding motif of Paul's whole life. His conclusion was this: "When it became clear that Jesus invested his whole life for me, I decided to invest my whole life for him."[86] Are the driving forces in our lives as clear to us?

Christ has risen

This is the third great theological conviction of the apostle. Paul put it very simply: If Christ had not been raised, then neither our preaching nor our faith would mean anything.[87] For Paul, everything stands or falls with the resurrection. If Jesus were still in the grave, he couldn't be anything more than a good man, perhaps a great prophet, to hold in our memories. But Jesus lives. Jesus is God's Son. God raised him from death. Death did not have the last word. Evil did not conquer. That's why Paul cries out for joy: "Death itself is defeated! The victory is complete!"[88] And that is why the resurrection itself became the great turning point, the new chapter in God's *Shalom* project.

The resurrection was and is the guarantee that the new era has truly begun. Never before had God intervened in this way in human history. God's power had never before been so clearly demonstrated. What had begun with Jesus was something totally new. Jesus was the first of a new humanity. Jesus was a prototype, as it were, of the new human person. And those who follow Jesus will go the same way Jesus went, through death to a new life. And not only in the future. The one who trusts in Jesus begins to experience the new resurrection life already.

Paul and the other apostles saw it absolutely clearly: Jesus brought time itself to a turning-point. He became the center of history. In Jesus, God has joined humanity, drawing closer to humanity than ever before. On him, the judgment that was to fall on rebellious humanity has already fallen. In him, the victory has been won over all principalities and powers, indeed even over death itself. With him, everything begins anew. A whole new foundation has been laid for God's *Shalom* project.

But one thing has not changed. God is still seeking people who will, of their own free will, return to God and become God's co-workers.

To Paul it was clear: those who have come to understand that, in Jesus, God's very life was invested for us, have no choice but to invest their whole lives for God in return.

Have we grasped that?

---

81 See, for example, the Parable of the Vineyard Workers (Matthew 21:33-39).
82 Colossians 2:15.
83 Mark 10:45.
84 1 Corinthians 15:3.
85 See 2 Corinthians 5:14, 21.
86 2 Corinthians 5:14ff.
87 1 Corinthians 15:14.
88 1 Corinthians 15:54ff.

For further reflection

1. "In Jesus Christ, God became a human." What does this sentence mean to me? Is there a way to clarify the meaning of this in my own words? What does that mean for my own life?

2. "Jesus died for me." What does this sentence mean to me? Is there a way to clarify the meaning of this in my own words? What does this mean for my own life?

3. "Jesus Christ rose again and lives." What does this sentence mean to me? Is there a way to clarify the meaning of this in my own words? What does this mean for my own life?

4. Am I so moved by the above claims that I can reach the same conclusion Paul reached, namely: "Since Christ gave up his life for me, I now choose to give my life entirely to him"? Do the two phrases, "Christ for me" and "I for Christ" fit together in my life? Or do I not make a connection between them?

5. What would I like to say very personally to Jesus Christ after all these considerations? Do I want to give thanks? Confess? Make a decision?

Dear Monica and Peter,

Remember how my presentation of Jesus in chapter 11 raised a lot of questions for you? With this chapter, I believe that the scales have been balanced again, haven't they? The picture of Jesus that this chapter presents looks a lot more like the one church tradition has usually handed down to us.

Yet when I read your letter, I think I detected that you were doing more than merely nodding in agreement. My encouragement that you formulate some of the core teachings about Jesus in your own words seems to have left you shaking your heads. You, Monica, give me the impression that this all seems like a bunch of academic theology, not the sort of thing that could ever touch the heart. You are puzzled that this seems to have moved Paul so deeply. Your reflections point to one of the central aspects of the Christian faith, something important enough to explore a bit more.

There are, first of all, some historical facts to consider: Jesus lived on earth and claimed to be the authentic witness sent from God the Father in heaven. The disciple community was united in its conviction and testimony that in Jesus of Nazareth, no less than the eternal God had come to be present among us. This Jesus died. Both Jesus himself and the early church confessed that this death was to be understood as a self-sacrifice, bringing about reconciliation with God. Then Jesus was raised from the dead, an event that both Jesus and his apostles interpreted as the beginning of a new creation. For the early church, these historical experiences, interpreted through the lens of their Old Testament faith, constituted irrefutable evidence that God was at work. Everything was now being changed. A new era in salvation history had begun.

And for us? Well, for us this all seems old hat sometimes. It's not the sort of thing that convinces us, lights a fire in us, transforms our lives. In fact, many of the theological claims that are made about these experiences have just the opposite effect. They are more likely to create intellectual difficulties for people today. God has become a human? How could that possibly be? Was Jesus really God, or was Jesus really a man, or was he somehow both? And what's the point of a sacrificial death? And was it really necessary for the Son of God to be sacrificed so that God would be appeased? A difficult concept indeed. And what exactly happened at the resurrection? Was there even a literal resurrection?

I think the German theologian Helmut Thielicke was right in what he said to his theology students. He observed that theological God-talk very quickly shifts from second-person speech to third-person speech, from "you" to "he," from talking *with* God to talking *about* God, from the nearness of a personal relationship to the distance of an object of study.

All the historical events surrounding Jesus of Nazareth, all those events that happened 2000 years ago, considered from the Old Testament Jewish perspective, say something very important to us: God is for us; God is faithful; God has drawn near; God has opened the way back to God; God forgives us our unfaithfulness; God never gives up on the great project; God will let us participate in the future that is becoming reality.

Sometimes there is not much else we can do but look at Jesus and thank him for showing us in the flesh that God loves us. The details of the incarnation, the logic of his substitutionary death, what was actually involved in the resurrection . . . these may well remain, to some extent, mysteries.

I wish you an "aha" experience, one that moves you deeply, as you continue to consider Jesus—with your understanding, but also with your inner vision and your praying heart.

Shalom,
Bernhard

14.
The mystery

Time to clear the air

Paul paced restlessly in his room. His face was twisted. Was the great apostle angry? It certainly looked that way. At a writing desk sat Paul's scribe, dipping a feather pen into the ink. Paul dictated: "I'm astonished at you. It was through the good news of Christ's grace that God drew you into this new life. And so quickly you turn your back on God who called you? There are people among you who are confusing you, trying to pervert the good news of Jesus. A curse on those who preach a different gospel than the one you already received!"[89]

What in the world happened here? What had gotten Paul so worked up? Why this thunderstorm let loose on the churches in Galatia? Obviously, there was a lot at stake. There was indeed, as a closer look reveals.

The big problem

The leaders of the young church had come to loggerheads. They had all been in agreement—Jesus was the Messiah and the new age of salvation had dawned. And everyone was in favor of the mission to the non-Jewish population, something that had not been all that self-evident at first. But then a major disagreement over the importance of Jewish traditions for the new believers came to light.

On one side were the very conservative Jewish Christians. Later, Paul called them Judaizers. In their minds, the renewed people of God were Jewish. God was at work among the Jews. Now, of course, the non-Jews could join them. Indeed, they were heartily welcomed to join. But if they wanted to join, they had to accept the Jewish traditions and laws, just as had always been the case for Jewish proselytes. In particular, they had to be circumcised and had to hold to the Jewish food laws. These Jews were clear about one thing: Anyone who wanted to become a Christian had to become a Jew first.

When these Jews learned that Paul was preaching the Gospel to non-Jews, and that they were responding and becoming disciples of Jesus Christ, receiving the Holy Spirit and founding churches—and all that without being circumcised—they became furious with Paul. Paul was severely opposed in Jerusalem at the end of his first missionary journey. And behind Paul's back, these Judaizers from Jerusalem started visiting the churches in Asia Minor, trying to persuade them that they would indeed have to be circumcised.

That explains Paul's anger. Paul was a great thinker and theologian, not to mention a fiery missionary. He grasped at once that this was no small matter. The first thing to do was to respond immediately. This had to be stopped as quickly as possible, lest a great deal of damage ensue. And Paul was very clear about the bottom line: One does not have to become a Jew to be a Christian. The entrance requirement for the people of God is faith in Jesus alone, nothing more! Add anything to that and it is a step backwards, a twisting of the good news of Jesus, a false gospel. Paul's letter was his first step in setting the threatened churches straight about this.

The second thing to be done was to work at reaching a consensus on this issue. And so a conference was called in Jerusalem. There the question was discussed at length and examined from all angles. Finally, the gathered body came to see things Paul's way. And that in itself represented a major breakthrough in the unfolding of God's great project. Now it could truly move beyond the confines of Judaism and expand among all the peoples of the earth.

But there was still a problem. At least for the theologian Paul it was a problem. What was the appropriate theological basis for their new consensus? How exactly was one to understand the relationship between Jews and non-Jews in the new people of God? How was the whole Old Testament to be understood? Figuring all of this out was then (and continues to be) a major theological challenge, one taken up by Paul in his letters to the Romans and to the Ephesians. Indeed, Paul's contributions in these letters are what truly define him as a great missionary to the non-Jewish world and a significant theologian in the early church.

The mystery

In several places Paul writes about the "mystery of Christ" that has been revealed to him. Whenever he speaks of it, he is referring to the fact that non-Jews (sometimes called Gentiles)[90] are now, through Jesus Christ, full participants in God's project.[91] Paul describes this mystery most fully in the letter to the Ephesians.[92] He sees the New Testament church as a new humanity[93] in which people are reconciled to God and also to each other. They are God's new *Shalom* people. And what is so marvelous is that this new "people of God" no longer remains limited to one ethnic group (the Jews). Rather, people out of all nations, ethnic groups, races, and cultures are brought together and reconciled. In fact, even more is happening. Men and women, masters and slaves, parents and children—are all being brought together and reconciled into one new humanity.⁹⁴ And all of that, says Paul, Jesus Christ has accomplished. Jesus is the ultimate peacemaker, bringing us back to God and into a new relationship with each other.

In the church, we see the beginnings of this new *Shalom* people. That is the incredible vision God gave to Paul.⁹⁵ And it is this *Shalom* people, this new community, that Paul also calls "the body of Christ." The community of Christ is the "embodiment" of Christ in the world. Paul did not proclaim an absent Christ; for Paul, Christ is present. Wherever people confess Christ and live in reconciled relationships with each other, Christ becomes visible. This is Christ's "body" in this world. This is God's project.

This is also why Paul got so defensive whenever people tried to persuade non-Jews to submit themselves to the Jewish law. God's project was at stake! Such persuasion was an attack against the body of Christ. In fact, whenever there was dispute, injustice, or especially an effort to divide the community of Christians into parties, Paul got zealous. God's project was at stake!

Christ did not only experience the full judgment on rebellious humanity. Christ did not only bring about reconciliation with God. Christ was not only the first member of the new humanity to be raised from the dead. Christ's work involves more than all of these; Christ is the founder of a whole new human race, a new human race in which all the dividing walls—cultural, national, or racial—are broken down. Even the walls of tradition that divide people are torn down in Jesus. God has established this new worldwide humanity as a sign to the rest of the world that God's *Shalom* project is being fulfilled.

With that in mind, how can Christians within the worldwide body of Christ still tolerate racism, nationalism, and an egotistical attitude to their own cultures? How can Christians continue to fight wars against each other, motivated by the interests of their national or ethnic identity?

Have we grasped what it means to be part of God's new humanity? Paul called it a mystery, revealed to him by God. Maybe our eyes need to be opened as well to see the mystery.

---

89 Galatians 1:6-9.

90 The Greek term *ethné*, which Paul uses here, is the usual New Testament technical term for non-Jewish peoples. Sometimes it is also translated as "nations" or "Gentiles," though these terms can be easily misunderstood today.

91 Romans 16:25ff; Ephesians 3:3-6; Colossians 1:26; 4:3.

92 Ephesians 2:11-22.

93 The new human (or "the new man") is used here as a collective term (new humanity), just as in Genesis 1(see comments on this in Chapter 3 of this book).

94 Ephesians 5:21-6:9; Galatians 3:26-29; Colossians 3:9-11.

95 In Ephesians 3:3-6 Paul emphasizes that this new insight was granted by revelation.

For further reflection

1. What does it mean to say that the church is a new humanity, in which reconciliation and peace are already breaking through, right in the middle of a fallen and torn world? Do I understand and experience church like this? Is that what I wish for the church?

2. How important in my thinking and in my life are issues related to the unity and reconciliation of all Christians?

3. How high a priority is it for me to live in reconciled relationships with sisters and brothers? Where should I be taking concrete steps toward reconciliation?

4. What do these considerations have to say about whom I define as an "enemy," how I treat foreigners, and how I respond to racism, war, and military service?

5. Where are there still separated and/or unreconciled groups, such as Jews and Gentiles, masters and slaves, males and females, in today's church?

6. What do these considerations do to me? Do they raise new questions? Do they lead me to make decisions? To speak to God in prayer?

Dear Monica and Peter,

Apparently your home fellowship group had another lively (or maybe even agitated!) discussion, as you responded to the chapter on "The mystery." You are wondering whether the problem of Judaizers is in any way relevant to what is happening in the contemporary church. Your group seems not to agree about this.

I believe this issue is absolutely relevant today. Just think for a moment about the influence of the culture around you on the visible expressions of your Christian faith. What are the forms of your prayers? What kind of dress code do you expect people to follow when they gather for Sunday services? What is the order of worship in your church services? What is the most common music style? What does your church building look like? In all these matters, what is essential to the Gospel and what is simply part of the culture?

When we as Christians from one culture interact with people of another culture, and invite them to follow Jesus, what do we expect from them? What must they do to become Christian? To be accepted as truly Christian, do they have to pray as we do? Wear similar clothing styles? Adopt our religious language? The style of our services? Our music? Our church architecture? For hundreds of years Western missionaries assumed so. We have only recently truly realized that it is completely acceptable if the Gospel takes on very different forms in different cultures, and that Christians in one culture have no right to prescribe the "right" Christian forms for another culture. Paul was already fighting this battle almost 2000 years ago.

What's more, the boundaries between cultures are not only between East and West, or between North and South; they run right through our own countries—between young and old, between rich and poor, between urban and rural, between men and women, between traditional Christian churches and secular society. The question must be asked over and over again: Are we seeking to convert people to our way of being Christian or to Jesus Christ and to God's project?

I wish you fruitful discussions as you continue to work out the practical implications of Paul's insights!

Sincerely,
Bernhard

15.
Caesar's competition

Uproar in Thessalonica

An outraged mob dragged a group of Christians to the city officials, shouting: "These people are causing trouble all over the world! They are defying Caesar's decrees and claiming that there is another king—Jesus."[96] Now this must have surely been a misunderstanding. Jesus couldn't really have been competition for Caesar, could he? Could a handful of Christians really cause trouble all over the world? Now of course the early church was calling Jesus "Lord." But we do this as well when we pray, sing songs, or recite confessions. This is not what revolutions are made of, is it?

Jesus Christ is *Kurios*

In the New Testament texts where English translations have the word "Lord," the original Greek used the word *kurios*. This was a highly explosive term in the 1st century. The Jews used this term to refer to their God, *Jahweh*. But there was more to it. In the Roman empire, *kurios* was also the title given to the emperor in Rome. What a provocation when the first

Christians called Jesus of Nazareth, *kurios*. Indeed, the outraged mob in Thessalonica understood clearly what was going on: Paul was traveling throughout the known world, proclaiming someone else as *kurios*, someone other than the emperor in Rome. We need to look closely at what Paul meant by that claim.

Victor over all principalities and powers

Paul's world was influenced and directed by many "powers." Of course, ours is as well. For example, religions claim the allegiance of people. With their legalisms, rituals, and required sacrifices, they put people in bondage. Political powers rule the world. Tyrants and despots, state systems and public officers rule over people and require them to submit. Philosophies strongly influence people's lives. They say that people find truth in the arts and sciences. There are all kinds of popular religious ideas, superstitions, and other influences that create fear and control lives.

Paul used terms like "principalities" and "powers" to speak about these sorts of influences on human life. And Paul knew as well that behind these power structures that he could see and experience, there were also forces of evil at work. Despite all their claims to contribute to human salvation, they actually enslaved people. Is it any different today? And what does all this have to do with Jesus?

Here Paul makes a resounding declaration: Jesus has publicly exposed all the powers. In their response to Jesus they have exposed their true natures. Jewish religion, Greek philosophy, the power of the Roman emperor—all of these played a significant role in the murdering of God's Son. And in doing so they revealed the true nature of their godless power. But

Jesus won the victory over them all. Their power was broken. Jesus' life, death, and resurrection are a triumphant victory march over all the powers and authorities.[97]

The powerful and liberating good news of the New Testament is precisely this: Those who have come to Jesus have been set free from the stranglehold of the principalities and powers and have been transferred into Christ's Kingdom.[98] Those who know Christ no longer have any ultimate allegiances to any other powers in heaven and on earth. Now their worship and honor belong to one *kurios* alone, the Lord Jesus. They have only one confession: Jesus Christ is *kurios!*[99]

Jesus Christ or Caesar?

According to Paul, this confession had implications for Christians' relationships to the Roman emperor. Governments belong to the powers and authorities.[100] Now of course God can still use these powers and authorities in working out the various aspects of God's project. Even the powers are not finally in control. God is still Lord of history.[101] But it is also true that the powers seek to control and dominate people, leading them away from God. For Paul, and for Peter as well, this meant that Christians must set some concrete priorities. We owe government officials respect and honor. Paul calls Christians to be appropriately "integrated" into the political state. But their *kurios*, their Lord, their final authority, is no longer the emperor of Rome; only Jesus is Lord. Our full and final obedience belongs to Jesus.[102]

Once more, the Thessalonian mob sensed what was happening. A preacher was traveling around the empire, proclaiming a different *kurios*. The old lords had reached the end of their tenure. Religions, superstition, philosophies, and political officials had served their terms; they were now removed from office. Their supposed omnipotence didn't turn out to be all that powerful. Jesus exposed and conquered them. And now God invites people to be set free from old fetters and chains and to come and find freedom in the kingdom of love that *Kurios* Jesus is establishing.

The King and his citizens

In the Old Testament, God wanted to be present in the gatherings of the people. So also now in the New Testament era, *Kurios* Jesus wants to meet with his people. And just as Jesus' Lordship was expressed in the political language of the day, so also political language of the day was used to characterize the church. When a king gathered his citizens, they were called his *ekklesia*. So also the church is the gathering together of those who have been called out of the kingdom of darkness and brought into the Kingdom of Jesus. That is the New Testament "people of God." And Jesus wants to meet regularly with the citizens to talk together about life in the Kingdom.

In the gathering, the *ekklesia* will express their worship, praise, and thanksgiving to the *kurios*. The *ekklesia* will listen to the instructions of the *kurios*. The *ekklesia* will celebrate the presence of the *kurios*. We call these gatherings "worship services." Of course Jesus doesn't actually show up in person. But he is present in the Spirit. His word is alive and well in the gathering. And the gathered community often celebrates the "meal of the Lord" as a sign of Jesus' Lordship, his presence, and his future coming. It is a "meal for the King," celebrated as a foretaste of the final banquet that will take place when King Jesus returns.

Preparing for a state visit

The *kurios* is coming again! "Lord, come soon," the early church prayed.[103] And that is exactly what Jesus promised to do. Some day he will return to fully and finally establish his reign. What a great reception that will be. The king's *ekklesia* rejoices already as it looks forward to that day. And again Paul borrows picture language from his political environment to describe this experience. He speaks of the *parousia* of the *kurios*. This language was used for the arrival of a king for an official state visit. In precisely this way, *Kurios* Jesus will one day come again. And, of course, when an official state visit took place, the people prepared a magnificent reception. Citizens of the city marched out to greet the coming king, and the king entered the city in the midst of the celebrating crowds. In similar terms, Paul describes the arrival of the Lord.[104]

Those of us living at the beginning of the third millennium ask the same questions the early church did. Who is our Lord? Which "powers" influence our lives? To whom or what do we "bow the knee"? From what do we also long to be set free? And now, just as then, people are invited to be transferred from those kingdoms controlled by the "powers" into the kingdom of Jesus' love. And these same people are still invited to serve *Kurios* Jesus with their whole hearts and lives.

96 Acts 17:1-9.
97 Colossians 2:15.
98 Colossians 1:13.
99 Philippians 2:10-11.
100 Romans 13:1 uses the term *exousia* (power, authority) to refer to government authorities.
101 Romans 13:1, 4 are to be interpreted in the light of Isaiah 44:28-45:5; Jeremiah 27:6; 43:10, etc. Political authorities, no matter how godless they may be, can still be used by God to accomplish divine purposes. However, this does not mean that the political authorities thereby gain a godly authority.
102 Romans 13:1-7; 1 Peter 2:17; see also Acts 4:19; 5:29.
103 1 Corinthians 16:22; Revelation 22:20.

104 1 Thessalonians 4:17. This text which is sometimes interpreted as the "rapture" of the church, should, in my opinion, not be interpreted as a literalistic journey to meet the Lord "in the air." It would be a mistake to use this text to speculate about he exact nature of the events that will happen when the Lord returns.

For further reflection

1. Where and how do I experience the claim of various "powers" in my life? How do I deal with them?

2. What does Jesus' victory mean to me personally? Does it have specific concrete effects on my life?

3. Where have I experienced liberation from the influence of "powers and authorities"? Where do I still long for such liberation?

4. What is my attitude to those in authority over me? Are there situations in which I sense the conflict between that which earthly authorities demand of me and what Christ wants from me? When I do, how do I respond?

5. In what kinds of situations would I like to increase my commitment to resist the pressure of worldly authorities in order to serve the Lord Jesus with an undivided heart?

Dear Monica and Peter,

Well, what can I say? Your last letter was loaded with questions and critical objections. Between the lines I detect some reproaching as well. In your opinion, I've turned Jesus' victory into something that is far too political. You are wondering how I could discuss this topic and not even talk about demonic powers. And besides, Paul did tell us to submit to the political authorities, didn't he? You don't think that I'm convinced we should. And you think the Gospel is to be understood spiritually, not politically. You especially want me to say more about the meaning of Romans 13:1-7.

In Romans 13 Paul is indeed writing about government authorities. And there he deliberately uses some of the same terminology that is used elsewhere to discuss various kinds of rulers and authorities, principalities and powers, rulers of the age, etc. According to Paul, governmental power falls into the same category as other worldly structures like culture, religion, and philosophy. All of these are "systems" in which humans (and for that matter the Christian church) live. All of these "worldly systems" are aspects of our life on earth. And God is ultimately Lord over these as well. God can use them to bring the world toward its divine destiny. And in this respect, governmental power can also be God's servant (compare Isaiah 44:28-45:5; Jeremiah 27:6; 43:10).

The church must also find its proper place within these world systems. "Submission" cannot be understood as absolute obedience to worldly authorities, regardless of what they require of us. In fact, the verses that immediately precede Paul's instructions in Romans 13 show us where our primary loyalty is: As Christians we are to live our lives fully dedicated to God, and not let the world squeeze us into its own mold (Romans 12:1, 2). We are to love all people. We are not to take revenge, but rather to bless our enemies. We are to conquer evil by doing good. We are not to adopt the methods of those who are evil (12:9-21). So when political authorities demand of us something which is not consistent with the ethics of Jesus, they have no divine authority to demand our submission.

Paul was calling the Christian church to reject the methods of violent resistance, i.e. rebelling against political authorities and trying to set up a "Christian state." On the contrary, Christians were and are to be integrated into the ordinary systems of this world. And they are to do that in such a way that they give to each one "what is their due" (13:7). That means, of course, that God is always in first place and deserves our full honor. Governmental systems receive only a relative "honor," expressed for example in the paying of taxes (compare 1 Peter 2:17).

In broad strokes I would portray the political dimensions of the church like this. The people of God is a true "people group" living in and among other people groups and nations of this world. We are "among" the nations and integrated into this world, but we live according to different values and principles.

Whereas virtually all of this world's people groups will put their national interests in first place, God's people represent an international people group crossing the lines of culture, ethnicity, and nationhood. Our primary allegiance is to God and to God's "international people group." As a result we will support and serve our own national interests only to the extent that these do not come in conflict with our primary allegiance. When we truly live this way, we as a Christian church are certainly also a political entity. There are inescapably political dimensions to being the Christian church, if we are the church according to biblical norms.

So now I am curious how you will respond to my additional comments, personally and in your discussion group. I look forward to your responses.

Sincerely,
Bernhard

16.
But . . . ?!

Too optimistic?

Are we being a bit too optimistic? God's project! New
person! New humanity! Reconciled people! People becoming God's willing co-workers! God's reign has begun! Jesus
has won the victory over all the evil powers!

Take a look around. A glance at the daily paper will be
enough. Scan your neighborhood. Look in the churches, for
that matter. Look back at church history. Maybe we don't
even need to look *around*. A glance at our own lives should
be sufficient to show that the goal has never been reached.
Where's the new person? Where is the new humanity?
Where is God's reign breaking through? What's all this
about God's project?

Before we label Paul & Company just a bunch of fanat-
ics and idealists, we ought to listen more carefully to exactly what they were saying and writing. I think we'll be
amazed at how realistic they really were. Let's take, for
example, the eighth chapter of the book of Romans. There
Paul writes that the new world being born is still in the
delivery stage. This picture drawn from human experience
is designed to make three things clear.

The new has begun

The picture of labor and childbirth indicates clearly that something new has begun. New life has been conceived. A new beginning is already underway. And Paul is just as certain that the new era of salvation has also begun. For Paul there is solid evidence of this:

1. Jesus is the promised Messiah. The resurrection is God's impressive evidence. Lots of eyewitnesses could verify that Jesus was truly raised from the dead. So there is now no doubt: The new humanity has begun. Jesus, the first of the new creation, is alive.[105]

2. Because Jesus lives, his life and his death can be seen in a new light. It is God's own life, given freely for the redemption of humanity. The judgment on humanity has been borne by Jesus.

3. Last but not least, the end-time Spirit has been poured out. Pentecost was the visible sign. As a result of God's great heavenly intervention, people were changed and united as the new people of God.

So Paul can confidently claim: The new has begun. We live because of Easter; we live the life of the resurrection. So Christians know that the morning is dawning, even if it is still dark.

The new is not fully present

Paul is equally clear about the other side of the coin: We have not yet reached the goal. The picture of labor and child-birth also captures the truth that the birth process can be very painful. The new does not arrive in the blink of an eye, and it does not come in its final form right away. You can't have everything in an instant. The birth of a new world is a process.

This is true for the individual: Though we are already reconciled to God through Christ, the renewal of our lives can be a painful experience. We as individuals do not become fully renewed all at once.[106] And this is also true for the community of believers: Though in Christ we are a new reconciled humanity, the realization of this new humanity can be a painful process. Communities also do not become fully renewed all at once.

The goal is in sight

Paul's faith was stamped with this conviction. He was certain that the new had already begun. And he was equally certain that it would one day reach its final goal. The picture of childbirth applies here as well. Paul also used the image of a down payment. A down payment is the guarantee that the full price will eventually be paid. Paul understood the gift of the Holy Spirit as the guarantee of the fulfillment yet to come.[107] This is the Christian hope, the confident assurance that the fullness of God's Kingdom is on its way. The life of the Christian in the present is influenced by this hope for the future. We live in the tension of a hope guaranteed, but not yet fulfilled.

Christian hope is not the same as holding on to utopian dreams; it's not simply building castles in the air "by faith" with no foundation in reality. True Christian hope is living today in the present, yet it is being directed by the future world that has dawned with the coming of Jesus.

Christians have not always managed to live in this tension, keeping the two polarities in balance. Often the old world has become so dominant in Christians' thinking that the experiences of Easter and Pentecost are all but forgotten. And when this happens, Christians simply adapt their lives to the realities of the old world. They no longer live as though the new world has dawned. They no longer trust in the power of the resurrection and they experience little or no evidence that the new age has dawned. They no longer trust in the power of the Spirit, and they experience little or no evidence of the "already" that God has made available through the power of the Spirit.

There have always been Christian groups who fall to the other extreme. They believe they have already reached the goal. They want to have it all, and right now, too. If someone experiences conversion, then they are expected to be instantaneously and completely new. According to such thinking, all infirmities will be healed if we truly believe and pray correctly. All of God's gifts and blessings belong to us already. The fullness of salvation is offered to us; we need only to take it. It's a bitter experience to realize that pain and suffering do indeed still come into our lives.

Living and experiencing life as a sign

We dare not demand all or nothing. We live "between the times." Our present experience is characterized by "signs" of the fullness. That means that the new really has begun and that it can be experienced and seen, but only as a sign of what is still to come. Already we experience renewal by God's Spirit—not in its completion, but as a sign of what's to come. Already we experience that God heals people—not everyone, and not always instantaneously, but God heals as a sign of greater things to come. Already we get a taste of what it is like to be a fellowship of peace, a true body of Christ—not in its perfection, but as a sign of what fellowship will one day be. Already we celebrate in our gatherings our fellowship with the Lord, not as it will be in heaven, but as a sign of that. We live today according to the principles of the Kingdom of God—not perfectly, but as a sign.

How will the world ever be persuaded that God's great *Shalom* project is indeed something wonderful and worth pursuing, if Christians don't live in the old world as a sign that the new world is dawning?

---

105 1 Corinthians 15.
106 Though it is tempting at this point to quote 2 Corinthians 5:17, one must be careful not to misunderstand this verse. *Quantitatively* it is not true that everything has been renewed through Christ. Paul is rather saying that for those who believe in Jesus, something *qualitatively* new has dawned. And that applies both to personal renewal and to the reality of a renewed community, a new humanity.
107 Ephesians 1:14; Romans 8:11.

For further reflection

1. Where in my own life do I experience tension between the "new world" and the "old world"? Where do I experience the new? Where I am still caught up in the old? How do I deal with this?

2. In which direction am I most likely to become one-sided? Am I inclined to be dominated by the reality of the old world and lose sight of the new? Or am I inclined to suppress the reality of the old and live in the illusion that everything is made new?

3. In which areas of my life would I like to create greater opportunities for God's

power and love to be revealed as a sign of
even more to come? Am I ready to open
new areas of my life to God? Do I truly
expect that God is able to bring about
renewal and healing in my life?

4. In which areas would I be willing to take
concrete steps as a sign of the reality of
God in my life? What would be one concrete step I could take, enabling me to live
in this world now as a sign of the coming
Reign of God?

5. In which areas in my life and in the life of
my congregation would I like to learn to
endure a still imperfect situation and not
become disheartened in the process?

Dear Monica and Peter,

Many thanks for your perceptive questions: How radically different are we to be? Are we supposed to practice a "community of goods"? Should we support alternative Christian schools and businesses? How can we "live as a sign" while living in the midst of the institutions of our society?

The discussion in your group seems to have been very similar to what I have often experienced. Someone makes a very radical proposal. Others respond by claiming that the idea is totally unrealistic. And soon the "realists" have shot so many holes into what was originally a challenging proposal for real change, that nobody thinks the idea is worth pursuing at all anymore. And everyone resigns themselves to the status quo once again.

It's a common trap. It is so easy to play mental games with good ideas until we end up doing nothing about them. We need to take a closer look at some of these games:

1. One of them is played when we make a proposal so radical that we can quickly conclude that following through on it would be totally impossible. In other words, the proposal we have made is so unrealistic, we don't do anything at all. We do this, for example, in our responses to the environment. Shouldn't Christians, of all people, be committed to a lifestyle that respects

and cares for God's creation? And this raises questions about the exhaust fumes we produce, indeed with the very idea of driving our cars. Radical suggestion: As Christians we should try to live without cars. Counter-argument: Totally impossible. Bottom line: Well, we'll just have to leave things as they are.

2. A second crippling game is called legalism. If we want to think seriously about a responsible Christian ethic, then sooner or later we have to talk about concrete practical steps. What is our attitude toward money? What is our response to refugees or illegal immigrants? How should we care for the environment? What kind of marriage and family life is expected of us? How do we deal with "principalities and powers"? What are the right guidelines for dealing with the media? With rampant consumerism? And as soon as we start to make specific proposals for concrete action, the "champions of grace" speak up and in the name of "grace" fight against all the "legalistic ideas." Bottom line: Don't ever propose specific concrete actions; that would be inconsistent with the gospel of grace.

3. Sometimes we play the game of calculating the chances of success (or more likely of fail-

ure). What difference would it make anyway, given the magnitude of the world's problems? We start to talk about the millions of
starving people all over the world, while
spending a pleasant evening together as a
home fellowship group, well fed and enjoying
a beautiful home. What can we do about
world hunger? How can we share our food
with the world's poorest? Maybe we even
dream up some possible involvement, but
nothing concrete ever comes of it, especially if
someone in the group asks the question we're
all thinking: What good would our little con-
tribution make anyway? Bottom line: We
don't bother doing anything at all.

These are common responses and I'm sure you can
add your own examples. So what does this all have
to do with "living as a sign"? To live as a sign means
we are so enthusiastic about Jesus Christ and the
coming Kingdom of God that we can't help but be
influenced already by the Spirit of Jesus and his
Kingdom. Of course we won't be able to do it perfectly, but we will at least dare to take small concrete
steps in the right direction. We don't do it as a way
of earning salvation. And we're not overly consumed
with the question: Does it really make much difference? Rather we ask: What is consistent with the
Spirit of Jesus and the will of God?

To live as a sign ultimately means that we *already* begin to live differently, even though we know that it is *not yet* possible to do it perfectly.

Hang in there! And don't let the mental games we play hold you back.

My greetings,
Bernhard

17.
The goal

Where are we heading?

Not very many people today have rose-colored glasses when they look into the future. The reality of war, injustice, destruction of the physical environment, and so on, have put dampers on our dreams. We think, "Today we are standing on the edge of the precipice. Will we be one step farther ahead tomorrow?" The next steps taken in human history will be difficult ones, but they are decisive for our future. Many people have given up hope of a happy ending. Their motto is: Let's enjoy the life we have today; it's not likely to last very much longer. Others respond with impatience: The time is so short we have to do something immediately; maybe this world can yet be saved. Others are simply discouraged, hanging their heads and doing nothing at all.

Christians and the future

Then along come Christians, talking about a new creation. Christians claim to know that in the future a new world order is coming, characterized by righteousness, peace, and joy. And as we have seen, they are quite certain about this; after all, with the resurrection of Jesus this new world has already dawned for them, right in the middle of the old. For

Christians, one thing stands sure: The fulfillment of God's great *Shalom* project will one day arrive. But what exactly will this fulfillment be like?

The Bible speaks of many events that will happen as the end of human history draws near.[108] Many of these statements concern things that are beyond our experience and not easily described in words. That is why the Bible often uses picture language to describe them. And that makes it hard to know exactly how we should interpret them. Unfortunately, Christians have also fought a lot about the so-called "end times." That doesn't have to happen, however, if we interpret the pictures carefully and don't get into all kinds of fantastic speculation and predictions about the future.[109]

Jesus Christ is coming again

We looked at one of the pictures earlier: The arrival of a king making an official state visit, and his reception by the people. This picture speaks of the return of Christ. Christians do not anticipate that humans will put forth their best efforts and slowly but surely transform this world into a perfect society. But neither does the Bible predict a catastrophic ending to world history with no future hope beyond. No, the church awaits the appearance of the Lord. He will bring about the full and final form of God's Kingdom. This conviction shapes the way Christians live in the present. Someone put it this way: "The lords of this world come and go; our Lord just comes." And so we express our joyous assurance that the future destiny of the world will not be left to chance and to an unknown destiny. Believers belong to their coming Lord. The future belongs to them together.

The Antichrist and the tribulation of the church

The New Testament speaks in various places about the spirit of the antichrist, of antichrists, and of *the* Antichrist. The writers speak of these using the present tense.[110] We should be careful not to relegate the antichrist idea to the very last days.

Those who have confessed Christ have come to experience that there are indeed powers at work in this world that are against Christ. Indeed, all the powers of this world throughout world history that set themselves up against Christ and his kingdom are antichrist powers. Suffering and persecution for Christ's sake have often been the lot of Christians in this world, belonging to the very essence of their Christian lives. But the writers of Scripture see one thing very clearly: tribulation will increase at the end of time. Things will eventually "come to a head."

More than once in world history things have gotten so difficult for the church that people were sure the end was just around the corner. For this very reason we should be hesitant about any predictions about the imminent end. And we should be just as hesitant to begin identifying who the Antichrist must be. The church has often faced difficult times and seen in one dictator or another the face of the Antichrist. And indeed, there have been brutal rulers whose actions have clearly opposed Christ and his kingdom.

The church of Jesus Christ is called upon at all times and in all places to live in this world with eyes wide open, holding faithfully to Christ when others oppose him. The church has no need to hunt around for an antichrist. If the church's words and works clearly embody faithful allegiance to God's peace project and to the Prince of Peace in this often violent world, the church can count on resistance and opposition. And still Jesus' word stands: "In the world you face persecution, but take courage; I have conquered the world."[111] It will not be the *Anti*christ, it will be *Christ* who has the final word in world history.

A new heaven and a new earth

Our great destination, according to John, is the new creation, the renewal of heaven and earth.[112] Death will be overcome and there will be no more tears. A new Jerusalem will come down from heaven to earth. In this city of God, the peoples of the earth will live together in peace forever. This is, of course, picture language.

We cannot say exactly what the fulfillment of God's great project will look like. In any case, we should not imagine the sort of heaven where we do nothing but sit around in a city of gold, playing golden harps and singing endlessly. That is a caricature of the new creation. Still, the pictures want to communicate something. Central to the message is this: "See, I am making all things new!"[113] All misery, all pain, all calamity will be a thing of the past. The human community will be made whole. *Shalom* will become a reality among the peoples of the earth. Joy, peace, and righteousness will no longer be but a dream. God will be forever present among us. Creation itself will be renewed and delivered from the curse of exploitation. This will indeed be the fulfillment of God's *Shalom* project.

The last chapters of the Bible say something else just as clearly. Among those present in that holy city will be all those whose names have been written in the "Lamb's book of life," that is, all those who throughout history have made a life commitment to Christ and who have joined the community of Jesus' followers. These are the ones who, already in this present age, have responded to God's invitation and become co-workers in God's *Shalom* project.

God's *Shalom* Project

So what now?

What does all this mean for our lives today? Many Christians are fighting tooth and nail for a better world, as if the entire future of our planet depended on us. Others live almost indifferently, unconcerned about the world's great problems. They are certain that after the world meets disaster, God will come along and make it all new again.

What I read in the New Testament is something different than these extremes. Because we know that God has a project, because we know that the fulfillment of God's project began in earnest with the coming of Jesus, because we know that with Christ's second coming this project will be brought to completion, we are invited as believers and as the church to experience and to live out the reality of God's project now already. We do it with calmness, neither fighting desperately for its success, nor holding out any illusions that we can get the job done, for we know that Jesus is coming again and that the fulfillment of God's project is not ours alone to accomplish. But we also do it with conviction and enthusiasm, because Jesus has laid hold of our lives. We do it because the Spirit has planted in our hearts a vision for God's great *Shalom* project.

What a privilege to be invited into this project!

---

108 The theological expressions sometimes used are "the end"or "the last things" or "the end times." However, the New Testament word *telos* should not be understood strictly as a chronological reference to what happens at the very end of time. Words like "goal" or "fulfillment" capture the meaning better than the word "end."

109 We do not endorse a so-called "Dispensationalist" view of the end times (as developed by Darby and popularized through the Scoffield Bible). For literature on this, see the list of Readings.

110 For example, 1 John 2:18ff.

111 John 16:33.

112 Revelation 21. At this point people often bring up the matter of "the Millennium," the prophesied "thousand years of peace" understood as something like an intermediate stage between present world history and the final new creation. There are various theological viewpoints on the Millennium that cannot be fully discussed here.

113 Revelation 21:5.

For further reflection

1. What role do thoughts of the future, of the end of the world, and of eternity play in my faith and my thinking?

2. Does a biblical hope have a significant impact on my everyday life, or is it just a theoretical perspective on the future?

3. Do I want to change the world by means of human effort? Or am I inclined to sit back and wait for the world's demise and God's new creation?

4. On the basis of the texts discussed in this chapter, how would I formulate a Christian way of thinking about life in this world? What does this mean for the way I live my life? And in all this, what is the role of the church?

5. What are my thoughts and my feelings, now that I have made my way through the Bible, looking at God's plans and purposes for humanity? Did I gain helpful insights along the way? Did new questions arise in my mind? Did my faith change in any way?

Dear Monica and Peter,

I have your last letter here in front of me. Thank you for letting me know that you are thinking deeply about God's project and about your part. And your critical comments forced me to think through some of the issues more carefully and, wherever possible, to express my convictions more clearly. I see that I have undergone some changes along the way.

What has happened to you as a result of this study? In your last letter you wrote: "We can sense that a fire has been lit again. The Bible has come alive, and the message of this old book is gripping us once more. Being a Christian, or rather, being co-workers in God's project, is about the most fascinating thing we can imagine."

If that is what has come about through your study of this book, then it is clear that God's *Shalom* project is being fulfilled in the story of your lives as well.

All the best,
Bernhard

For Further Reading—
An Annotated Bibliography

An extensive bibliography which contains all sources used in the book is available on the Good Books website, www.goodbks.com.

A selected number of books are suggested for further reading:

Berkhof, Hendrik. *Christ and the Powers.* Scottdale, PA: Herald Press, 1977.

This study of Paul's concept of principalities and powers relates especially to Chapter 15 of this book.

Betz, Otto. *What Do We Know About Jesus?* Philadelphia, PA: Westminster, 1968.

This additional reading for Chapter 11 offers more information on the Gospels and the reliability of the biblical account.

Bockmühl, Klaus. *The Christian Way of Living: The Ethics of the Ten Commandments.* Vancouver, B.C.: Regent College Publishing, 1997.

This helpful companion to Chapter 7 interprets the Ten Commandments into the contemporary context.

Clouse, Robert (ed.). *The Meaning of the Millennium: Four Views.* Downers Grove, IL: InterVarsity, 1997.

This helpful additional reading to Chapters 16 and 17 compares four Christian theories on the end of the world (eschatalogy).

Driver, John. *Understanding the Atonement for the Mission of the Church.* Scottdale, PA: Herald Press, 1986.

In Chapter 13, several meanings of Christ's death are portrayed. This book gives more theological background and explores many more biblical images for the cross.

Eller, Vernard. *War and Peace from Genesis to Revelation.* Scottdale, PA: Herald Press, 1981.

This fascinating book tells the biblical story in a way similar to this book, yet focuses on themes of war and peace. It is an ideal supplement to this book.

Ewert David. *And Then Comes the End.* Scottdale, PA: Herald Press, 1980.

In Chapters 16 and 17 we explore the meaning of the "end times." Ewert's book is a fine and thorough exposition of almost all relevant biblical texts and themes.

Janzen, Waldemar. *Old Testament Ethics: A Paradigmatic Approach.* Louisville, KY: Westminster John Knox, 1994.

Biblical ethics can be derived from different types of biblical texts. We touch upon many in almost all the chapters. Janzen provides and gives more biblical background to the various paradigms of biblical ethics.

Kraus, C. Norman. *Community of the Spirit: How the Church is in the World.* Scottdale, PA: Herald Press, 1993.

This fascinating book on Pentecost, the Holy Spirit, and the church is a supplement to Chapter 12.

Kraybill, Donald B. *The Upside-Down Kingdom.* Scottdale, PA: Herald Press, 1994.

In several chapters we point to the fact that a way of life which follows God's project stands in contrast to much of human behavior and to many cultural values. Kraybill's challenging book deepens this idea.

Kreider, Alan. *Journey Toward Holiness: A Way of Loving for God's Nation.* Scottdale, PA: Herald Press, 1987.

Here is another book which tells the story of God's project through Scripture, this time focusing on God's plan to call a people that lives an alternative way of life.

Lind, Millard C. *Jahweh Is a Warrior—The Theology of Warfare in Ancient Israel.* Scottdale, PA: Herald Press, 1980.

In Chapter 7 we touch upon the difficult theme of war in the Old Testament but do not expand on it. This book introduces various aspects of the topic.

Lohfink, Gerhard. *Jesus and Community: The Social Dimension of Christian Faith.* Philadelphia, PA: Fortress, 1984.

Going beyond what we indicate in Chapter 11, Lohfink shows the roots of church, beginning with the Jesus community.

Sider, Ronald J. *Rich Christians in an Age of Hunger: Moving From Affluence to Generosity.* Dallas, TX: Word, 1997.

The prophets of the Old Testament, as well as Jesus, critiqued the social injustices of their times (Chapters 9 and 11). Sider gives an expanded picture of this prophetic view and relates it to contemporary issues.

Sider, Ronald J. *Christ and Violence.* Scottdale, PA: Herald Press, 1979.

In Chapters 11, 13, and 14 we speak about Jesus' role in God's *Shalom* project. Sider adds additional dimensions to this theme.

Yoder, John H. *The Politics of Jesus: Behold the Man! Our Victorious Lamb.* Grand Rapids, MI: Eerdmans, 1994.

In Chapter 11 we try to show that Jesus' life had socio-political relevance. Yoder's classic text provides the biblical and theological foundation for such a perspective.

Index of Scriptures

*(Page numbers where the Scripture verses can be found in **God's Shalom** Project follow the Scripture references.)*

God's *Shalom* Project

Matthew
    3:17—77
    4:17—78
    5:7—79
    5:13-16—79
    6:6-13—7
    10:17-19—87
    18:23-25—11
    21:33-39—95
    26:36-56—80
    27:39-44—80
    28:18-20—81
    28:19—86
    28:20—87

Mark
    1:14-15—78
    10:45—96
    14:36—80

Luke
    4:16—78
    4:18-19—93
    24:49—87

John
    4:34—77
    9:16—80
    10:19-21—80
    11:45-57—80
    13:34-35—79
    14:6—80
    14:16—87
    15:20—87
    16:33—133
    17:21—79
    18:1-19—80
    20:19—81
    20:21—86

Acts
    1:8—86
    2:1-13—87
    4:19—113
    5:29—113
    17:1-9—111

Romans
    8—120
    8:11—122
    13:1,4—113
    13:1-7—113
    16:25—105

1 Corinthians
    15—121
    15:3—96
    15:14—97
    15:54—97
    16:22—115

2 Corinthians
    5:14—96
    5:17—122
    5:21—96

Galatians
    1:6-9—103
    3:26-29—106

Ephesians
    1:14—122
    2:11-22—105
    3:3-6—105,106
    5:21-6:9—106

Philippians
    2:10-11—113

Colossians
    1:13—113
    1:26—105
    2:15—96,113
    3:9-11—106
    4:3—105

I Thessalonians
    4:17—115

I Peter
    2:17—113

I John
    2:18

Revelation
    21—132
    21:1—7
    21:5—132
    22:20—115

About the Author

Bernhard Ott was born in Switzerland where he lives now with his wife Margrit. They are the parents of four adult children. The Otts are members of the Evangelische Täufergemeinde Basel.

Ott's theological training is from the Theological Seminary Bienenberg, Switzerland (Diploma, 1977), Mennonite Brethren Biblical Seminary in Fresno, California (Master of Divinity, 1984), and the Oxford Centre for Mission Studies in Oxford, England (Ph.D., 1999).

Ott has taught at the Theological Seminary Bienenberg since 1980. He has been the Director of Studies there since 1984.

He has also taught extensively in Switzerland, Germany, and Paraguay.

About the Translator

Timothy J. Geddert is associate professor of New Testament at Mennonite Brethren Biblical Seminary, Fresno, California. He has authored a number of books including one on Mark's Gospel and, most recently, a book on Christian ethics.